Frederic Remington: The Writer

Twayne's United States Authors Series

Joseph M. Flora, Editor

University of North Carolina, Chapel Hill

TUSAS 716

FREDERIC REMINGTON, 1900
Courtesy Frederic Remington Art Museum, Ogdensburg, N.Y.

Frederic Remington: The Writer

Roscoe L. Buckland

Western Washington University

Twayne Publishers
New York

Twayne's United States Authors Series No. 716

Frederic Remington: The Writer
Roscoe L. Buckland

Twayne Publishers
1633 Broadway
New York, NY 10019

Library of Congress Cataloging-in-Publication Data
Buckland, Roscoe L., 1918–
    Frederic Remington : the writer / Roscoe L. Buckland.
        p. cm. — (Twayne's United States authors series ; TUSAS 716)
    Includes bibliographical references (p.) and index.
    ISBN 0-8057-1607-6 (alk. paper)
        1. Remington, Frederic, 1861–1909—Criticism and interpretation.
2. Western stories—History and criticism.   3. Frontier and pioneer life in literature.
4. West (U.S.)—In literature.   I. Title: Frederic Remington, the writer.
II. Title.   III. Series.
PS2695.R72 Z59 2000
818'.408—dc21   99-059565

10 9 8 7 6 5 4 3 2

Printed in the United States of America

To Barbara and Phil

Contents

Illustrations

Preface

In the public mind, Frederic Remington is the artist preeminent of the American West. Thus it comes as a surprise to today's readers to learn that Remington was a writer as well as an artist. In the 1880s Henry Harper and other editors sent him out west on commissions as an artist, doing illustrations of Indians, cowboys, and soldiers. Before long, Remington began to write as well as to illustrate. His lively, often humorous style was an immediate success. As a journalist he wrote more than 100 articles for the major magazines of the day, giving spirited accounts of his own observations and experiences. He also wrote a dozen short stories and two novels, all popular in their day.

A second surprise about Remington is that he did not live in the West, except for two years in Kansas as a young man. He was born in upstate New York and spent his professional life in New York City. His sojourns in the West were brief, albeit numerous. His years in Kansas were spent as a sheep rancher in Peabody and part owner of a saloon in Kansas City. Both enterprises failed, and what he saw after that of cowboys and ranching was as a guest, not an employee.

After a middle-class childhood in Canton and Ogdensburg, New York, Remington drifted through a series of jobs, knowing he wanted to be an artist but not having a clue how to go about it. At the Yale School of Fine Arts, he disliked the European tradition offered and did not stay the course. He was fascinated by the West, but ran through his inheritance from his father in his failed ventures in Kansas. When he came to New York City in 1885, he was broke and had to be subsidized by his family. After a short term at the Art Students League, where he made lifelong friendships, he gave it up to look for a way to make money. And make money he did. He sold some Western sketches to *Harper's,* and within a year he had become a highly paid illustrator of Western lore in major magazines.

Three figures dominate Remington's West: the soldier, especially the cavalryman; the Indian, whose culture fascinated him; and the cowboy, with special fondness for the Mexican vaquero. He hobnobbed with generals and with dashing young cavalry officers but paid tribute equally to the common soldier. He wrote about skirmishes with the

Indians and was close to the front at the battle of Wounded Knee in 1890.

The West was not his only subject. As a correspondent, he covered the notorious Pullman strike in Chicago in 1894, supporting the role of the army in maintaining order. After some years of eagerly hoping to find a "real" war, he covered the Santiago campaign in Cuba in the Spanish-American War and wrote movingly about it, having learned that modern warfare was brutal and ugly, not the dashing forays against noble Indians that he had pictured. He wrote about the sports he loved: hunting, fishing, canoeing, and camping, often treating them as pleasurable trials of physical endurance.

Theodore Roosevelt and Owen Wister are often cited with Remington as the trio of leading exponents of the American West. All three were personal friends as well as collaborators on various projects. Remington's friendship with Roosevelt began when he was asked to illustrate Roosevelt's *Ranch Life and the Hunting-Trail* (1888). They met and corresponded at intervals throughout the ensuing years, Roosevelt praising Remington's writing skills as well as his drawing. After the war in Cuba, Roosevelt persuaded Remington to paint the famous *Charge of the Rough Riders at San Juan Hill,* against Remington's protests that he had been in the area but had not actually seen the event.

Remington and Owen Wister met by chance while traveling in the Yellowstone Territory in 1893. Wister, whose first stories were just coming out in Harper's magazines, was impressed at meeting the now-famous illustrator, and for the next decade, they often collaborated. Remington illustrated many of Wister's stories, and Wister wrote copy for many of Remington's paintings and drawings. It was Remington who pressed Wister to write his essay "The Evolution of the Cow-Puncher," providing him with details of Western life. It was Wister's novel *The Virginian* (1902) that stirred Remington to compete by writing the novel he had been contemplating, *John Ermine of the Yellowstone* (1902). Both novels were best-sellers in their day, but Wister's has survived as the prototype of the classic Western.

Much of what Remington wrote reflected the attitudes of his time— the era that praised the strenuous life and cultivated the martial spirit— but unlike many of his contemporaries who wrote in platitudes, Remington wrote no cant. He does not praise the ennobling effect of sport; he was a man who simply enjoyed being bruised on the Yale football field, boxing in taverns, or keeping up with cavalry in the Southwest deserts. In what he wrote of soldiering and war, there is no flag-waving or talk of manifest destiny; he was a war lover who thought war was "the greatest thing men do," and he stated quite plainly that the work of soldiers and warriors was to kill or to die, until he saw the killing and the killed in Cuba.

Remington was a man of extremes. A huge man, boisterous and likable, always overweight but physically active, he could ride and romp with the hard survivors of the West that he called "men with the bark on." At the same time, he could debate with the artists, writers, and actors at the Players Club in Manhattan, and have restful days with old boyhood friends in upstate New York. He rose early, worked hard at both his art and his writing, "relaxed" with swimming, tennis, riding, and canoeing, and talked into the night—all of which required quantities of meat and potatoes and whisky. He was a man of boundless energy and confidence, an artist, sculptor, and writer constantly experimenting and looking for new material or reworking the old.

From all this he wrote rollicking tales of happy sportsmen, of men at war in north plains blizzards and Southwest heat, and finally of men dying sudden and lonely deaths.

In his final years, from 1902 until his untimely death in 1909 at the age of 48, Remington gave up writing and devoted himself to serious painting, and especially to his sculpture. Writing was always his secondary career. He was pleased at becoming a "real writer," when his work came out in book form, but he regarded himself always as an artist who happened to write, not as a writer who drew.

I am grateful to the following for permission to reproduce the illustrations in this book: to the Frederic Remington Art Museum in Ogdensburg, New York, for the photograph of Remington at his desk, writing, circa 1900; to the New York Metropolitan Museum of Art for the painting *Cavalry Charge on the Western Plains in 1860;* to the National Cowboy Hall of Fame, Oklahoma City, for *Cheyenne Buck;* and to Peggy and Harold Samuels for (1) *Black Water,* (2) *"I Will Tell the White Man How He Can Get His Ponies Back,"* and (3) *John Ermine.* I want to thank the staff of the Wilson Library at Western Washington University for their many services. Above all I want to express my indebtedness to my wife, Audrey Peterson Buckland. Without her encouragement the book would never have been completed; without her editing it would never have been ready for either the printer or the reader.

Chronology

1861   Born in Canton, New York, 4 October.

1875–1876   Attends Vermont Episcopal Institute.

1876–1878   Attends Highland Military Academy, Worcester, Massachusetts.

1878–1880   Attends Yale School of Fine Arts; plays varsity football on famous team of '79.

1880   Father dies.

1881   First trip to the West; visits Montana Territory. Sketch of a cowboy accepted by Harper Brothers.

1881–1882   Various office jobs.

1882   Age 21, comes into inheritance.

1883   Buys a sheep ranch near Peabody, Kansas.

1884   Ranch fails; becomes partner in a saloon in Kansas City. 1 October: Marries Eva Adele Caten at Gloversville, New York.

1885   Hardware business fails; returns to New York; end of his last residence in the West.

1886   9 January: First sketch credited with his name, on cover of *Harper's Weekly.* March: Joins Art Students League in Manhattan. First commission from Henry Harper to go west. Meets Lieutenant Powhatan Clarke and General Nelson Miles.

1887   Painting hung at the 29th Annual Exhibition of the American Water-Color Society. First published writing: "Coursing Rabbits on the Plains" (*Outing,* May). Meets Theodore Roosevelt while illustrating Roosevelt's *Ranch Life and the Hunting-Trail.*

1889   Painting, *Last Lull in the Fight,* receives second-place medal from American jury for Paris International Exposition; illustrates Longfellow's *Hiawatha.*

1889–1902   Writes and illustrates more than 100 articles for *Harper's* and other magazines, many recounting personal experiences in the West and elsewhere.

1890   Moves from Manhattan to large estate in New Rochelle called "Endion." Writes about and illustrates the battle at Wounded Knee.

1891   Elected Associate of the National Academy of Design.

1892   Travels abroad with Poultney Bigelow to Germany and Russia, Remington stopping in London on the return. Sees Buffalo Bill Cody's Wild West Show in London.

1893   Meets Owen Wister while traveling in the Yellowstone.

1894   Covers the Pullman strike uprising in Chicago.

1895   First book: *Pony Tracks,* collection of articles previously published by Harper. First bronze statue: *The Bronco Buster.*

1896   Sent by William Randolph Hearst to Cuba with Richard Harding Davis to try to meet insurgents; stopped by the Spanish.

1897   Hearst publishes sketches by Remington of appalling conditions in Cuba. First fiction, "The Great Medicine-Horse: An Indian Myth of the Thunder" (first Sun-Down Leflare story).

1898   *Crooked Trails:* anthology of *Harper's* articles. 21 April: War declared against Spain; Remington is correspondent in Cuba for both Harper and Hearst. "With the Fifth Corps" (*Harper's Monthly,* November), his account of the Santiago campaign. Rough Riders give Roosevelt a statuette of Remington's *The Bronco Buster.*

1899   Paints *Charge of the Rough Riders at San Juan Hill. Sun-Down Leflare:* Five stories previously published by *Harper's. Stories of Peace and War:* Three selections from *Harper's.*

1900   *Men with the Bark On:* Last anthology from *Harper's.* Honorary degree from Yale University as a distinguished pupil of the Art School. Buys Ingleneuk, an island on the St. Lawrence River, for a summer place.

1902 *John Ermine of the Yellowstone,* second novel, but published before *The Way of an Indian.*

1903 *John Ermine* produced as a play on Broadway.

1902–1909 Gives up writing to devote himself to serious development of fine art, both painting and sculpture.

1905 *The Way of an Indian,* first novel, written in 1900 but not published until 1905.

1908 *The Cowboy,* 12-foot bronze, unveiled at Fairmont Park, Philadelphia.

1909 May: Moves into new mansion in Ridgefield, Connecticut. 26 December: Dies from complications of appendicitis at age 48.

Chapter One
The Life

Frederic Sackrider Remington was born in Canton, New York, on 4 October 1861, the only son of Seth Pierre Remington and Clara Bascom Sackrider.[1] Both the Sackriders and the Remingtons were well-established families in the town, the Sackriders in the hardware trade, Grandfather Seth Williston Remington, a Universalist pastor.

At the time of Frederic's birth, his father was owner and editor of the St. Lawrence *Plaindealer* and postmaster for Canton. In December 1861 he joined the first United States Volunteer Cavalry for what was then called the "War for the Suppression of the Rebellion." As Major Remington of the 11th New York Cavalry, he served with distinction, gaining a reputation for gallant if sometimes reckless action. He was honorably discharged 11 March 1865. In civilian life he was addressed as "Colonel," a courtesy title that he carried well. He was a tall, lean man, an excellent horseman, sporting a dangling moustache and pointed "imperial" beard. He was gentlemanly in manner, yet a man with firm opinions freely and forcefully expressed. The Colonel became the model for the dashing cavalryman of Frederic's art and writing.

After the war, the Colonel resumed his career in journalism, was active in Republican party politics, and became a partner in a stable of racing horses, to the delight of his young son. In 1869 he was appointed Collector of United States Customs in Ogdensburg, on the St. Lawrence River near Canton, where he engaged in the mutually beneficial occupations of a country gentleman: politics, journalism, and horse racing.

Frederic was a physically active boy; Canton and Ogdensburg suited him well with their woods and streams for camping, fishing, swimming, and skating. He was a carefree, good-natured, pudgy but athletic, boisterous village boy, often the leader. In his quiet moments he drew pictures. At the age of 14 he was enrolled in the Vermont Episcopal Institute, where he hated the strict discipline. The following year he transferred to the Highland Military Academy in Worcester, Massachusetts, where he was distinguished for his size and strength and popular for his good humor and generosity. He sketched constantly, making car-

1

icatures of officers and teachers and decorating the pages of his friends' souvenir books.

Young Remington's love of drawing began early. He drew rough figures of contemporary adventure lore—Turks, Russians, Indians, soldiers, cowboys, and villainous types—but had no interest in society men and ladies. Although his first fondness was for art, his best school subject was English composition. Students at Highland were required to write an essay each week, a page of writing every day, and a letter every three days. His writing showed a keen ear for language, a lively style, and a sense of humor, but he never mastered punctuation or spelling. His letters and journals are replete with errors. He was proud of his name "Frederic" without the "k," but throughout years of correspondence with his friend Powhatan Clarke, he never managed to get the final "e" on his friend's name. Today he would probably have been identified as having some degree of dyslexia.

The Colonel hoped that his son might find a career in the army, but Frederic was a poor scholar, especially in mathematics. West Point was precluded. When Frederic left Highland, his father suggested that he go into journalism. Frederic himself, whose real desire was to study art, persuaded his father that at Yale he could learn both writing and art, and in 1878 he was enrolled in the Yale School of Fine Arts.

For the first time in Frederic's life the aspiring artist could devote himself entirely to the study of art and receive disciplined instruction in drawing and painting. Enthusiastic at first, he soon grew impatient with the still-life and classical European forms that dominated the curriculum. He wanted to paint figures in action.

What did interest the young Remington was the social life. As a student in the professional art school, he was not, strictly speaking, a "Yale man," but he soon made friends among the undergraduates and caught on quickly to the stylish clothes and the "old fellow" speech. By the time he went home for the summer of 1879 he could play the part of a Yale man on the streets of Canton, adding distinction to the family status.

With a paternal background of public life and a maternal background of successful business, young Frederic was expected to amount to something out of the ordinary if he applied himself as his father and uncles had done, but he showed little such inclination. In August of that summer he met Eva Adele Caten, who had come with her brother to attend St. Lawrence University, a rare opportunity for a girl at that date. The daughter of Lawton Caten, a railroad superintendent and coal merchant at Gloversville, New York, Eva was poised, intelligent, and attractive, and Frederic fell in love.

When he returned to Yale in the fall, he was increasingly bored with the technical aspects of his study but keen on sports. Varsity football was drawing large crowds, and when Remington was invited to join the team, he jumped at the chance. It was no mean distinction to have served on what became the legendary football team of '79, with Walter Camp as the immortal quarterback. Some years later, when Remington had become a popular figure, he wrote articles defending football against charges of brutality, stressing the heroic qualities of the game, opposing the namby-pambies who would emasculate it. In time, Remington as the battered but ebullient varsity rusher and associate of Walter Camp became part of the Remington legend, considerably embellished through retelling.

Yale also produced some valuable friendships. A Yale undergraduate named Poultney Bigelow was the editor of the *Yale Courant,* which published a Remington cartoon of a battered and bandaged football player, and their acquaintance led to future collaboration.

When the football season ended, Frederic went home for the Christmas holidays and never returned. Undoubtedly he had learned more than he cared to admit from his classes, but although Yale gave him an honorary degree in 1900, citing him as a most distinguished pupil of the Art School, the faculty at the time he was there did not regard him as a serious student.

In February 1880 Remington suffered the shock of the death of his beloved father. Two years earlier he had observed in letters to his mother and his Uncle Horace that his father was pale and thin. Now, at the age of 46, the Colonel had succumbed to tuberculosis, at a time when Frederic perhaps needed the parental counsel that his father might have given but that his mother could not supply. Frederic was much like his father in temperament: gregarious, good-natured, confident, opinionated, even reckless, whereas Clara Remington was quiet, cautious, restrained. Their relationship was uncongenial. In later years, when Clara married a man whom Frederic considered socially beneath her, they were permanently estranged.

The Colonel left a gross estate of almost $22,000, which Frederic and his mother were to share equally. With the interest on her share, Clara could live in modest comfort. Frederic received an immediate advance of about $770 for support; the rest he would receive on his 21st birthday, with two uncles—Horace Sackrider and Lamartine Remington—acting as executors.

Remington had no idea what he wanted to do. Pursuing further study of fine art did not interest him. The uncles provided him with a series of clerical jobs, none of which appealed. Appointed executive clerk in the governor's chambers, he moved to Albany, where he did make some effort at this job, since Eva Caten lived just 40 miles up the river. Eagerly, he pursued the courtship, but when, in August 1880, he wrote to her father asking his consent to their engagement, he was firmly, and understandably, rejected as being too young and having no certain prospects.

Dismayed at the rejection, Remington quit the job in the governor's office and did not stick for long to various posts provided by his uncles. They soon saw that he was going nowhere, and at last an agreement was reached. He would have six months of freedom to travel, after which he would return to Albany to a proper job. Without any clear goal, but with a boyish enthusiasm for exploring the wild West, Frederic set off on a trip to Montana Territory in August 1881, a journey that would ultimately determine his career.

Remington found the West an exciting place. He visited the battle-ground where just five years earlier Custer and his troops had been wiped out. There were Indians still carrying rifles, albeit confined to reservations. There were troops of cavalry and infantry on active duty, and freight wagons carried men and goods to cattle towns, mining towns, and army posts. Large-scale mining and the open-range cattle bonanza were in full swing, with town toughs and cowboys and rustlers. Remington was entranced, but if he thought of buying into a mine or a cattle ranch, his $10,000 inheritance would not have been enough.

The first hint of a career came in an offhand way. Somewhere in Wyoming he drew a sketch of cowboys on a piece of wrapping paper, stuffed it in an envelope, and mailed it to *Harper's Weekly*. Perhaps intrigued by the Wyoming postmark, the art director purchased the sketch, and it appeared in the magazine as a full-page illustration for an article about the Southwest, bearing the caption "Cow-boys of Arizona: Rousted by a Scout." Although redrawn by Harper's Western illustrator and credited as "Drawn by W. A. Rogers from a Sketch by Frederic Remington," it was Remington's first paid illustration and the beginning of what later became a long association with the house of Harper.

When he returned to Albany in October 1881 and dutifully took up a job in an insurance office, he must have harbored a hope that somehow he might find a quick fortune and fitting subjects for his art in the West. He wrote to his relatives that he was happy in clerical work and doing well at it, when in fact he spent much of his desk time drawing sketches of the other clerks. In the end, he left the job shortly after Christmas and dawdled at home in Canton until his 21st birthday, 4 October 1882, when he came into his full inheritance.

Now was his chance to go back to the West to make his fortune. In February 1883, the year Theodore Roosevelt bought a ranch in Weslin, Dakota, as an investment and a hunting lodge, Remington bought 160 acres near Peabody, Kansas, for a sheep ranch. By the end of May he had invested $7,750 of his inheritance in land, sheds, sheep, and horses. Sheep ranching was an investment he could afford, but it carried none of the romance of the cattle ranch and was regarded as beneath the dignity of the affluent easterners who glorified the cowboy. Theodore Roosevelt had been known to declare that "no man can associate with sheep and maintain his self-respect" (Samuels, 93). Moreover, the ranching was hard work, little of which could be done from the back of a horse. Remington assigned the drudgery to two hired men, and like many young men of means who came west to engage in cattle or sheep farming, he went on a rough Western holiday: horse racing, hunting jackrabbits, bronco riding, roping, boxing, and partying in the stockmen's club. Remington made a name for himself, especially in boxing, wrestling, and wild riding, in spite of his 250 pounds. He was already fighting his lifelong battle with weight, going on periodic diets but becoming an enormous man, remaining remarkably active in spite of his girth. He was tending the ranch with no more effort than he had earlier applied to school or to clerking, but he filled a sketchbook with drawings and covered the walls of his ranch buildings with sketches.

By the end of September Remington had invested his entire inheritance but had made no money. In the end, he sold his ranch—land, livestock, buildings, and equipment—for enough to recover all but $2,000 of his investment. Back home in Canton, he looked for someone to invest with him in another Western venture, this time in the hardware business in Kansas. Since the Sackriders had built their modest fortunes in hardware, his mother was pleased with this plan and agreed to lend him $2,000, which he said was needed for extra capital and which replaced the money he had lost in ranching.

While at Canton he renewed his proposal to Eva Caten, and her father now gave his consent, on condition of the young man's success in the hardware business.

In March of 1884 Remington went back to Kansas City with a partner and opened a shop dealing in iron, steel, and hardware. Kansas City was a bustling, growing city, and the business should have prospered, but the partnership lasted just one month, Remington claiming that the man had swindled him. However it came about, Remington lost $1,500 and his second Kansas venture failed. At about the same time in 1884, Theodore Roosevelt, following the deaths of his wife and mother and a setback in Republican party politics, went west to manage his Dakota cattle ranch, into which he would sink $50,000 in the next two years.

With the $7,500 remaining, Remington gave himself up to enjoying the good life. He posed as an Eastern journalist who had spent time on a Western ranch; he had the leisure and the money to engage in boxing, riding, poker, and drinking. One pleasure—the women of Kansas City— seems not to have interested him. He appeared to be, as he wrote to Eva, a one-woman man, an attitude he maintained to the end of his life.

In June he became a silent partner in a saloon, spending most of his time sketching the patrons of the place. The business was doing well, and Remington made a down payment on a house in a prosperous residential area and described himself as an iron broker operating out of his home. Thus set up, he returned to New York, and on 1 October 1884, he and Eva Caten were married.

Arrived in Kansas City, Eva evidently found Frederic a playful and affectionate young husband, but she could not help noticing that no brokerage business entered or left their home and that he returned in the evenings with whiskey on his breath and sketches obviously drawn in a saloon or a pool hall. What she saw of Kansas City was not what she was looking for when she left Gloversville, and Eva went home early for the Christmas holidays and did not return.

Stirred to action, Remington now turned to painting, this time with a purposeful, self-disciplined effort to become a professional artist. He bought supplies and worked in oils and watercolor, using Western subjects. When a few paintings were sold for good prices, and *Harper's Weekly* accepted another illustration, Remington was convinced his career was on its way. Soon, however, he had run through most of his money. After a sketching excursion into New Mexico, he was back in Kansas City, penniless and hungry. He borrowed money for train fare, and in September he arrived in New York City. His two years in Kansas were the only time in his life when he lived in the West. He returned often for short periods but remained a New Yorker, living in or near Manhattan.

That same summer Owen Wister had taken a rest cure on a Wyoming ranch. By September he was enrolled at Harvard to begin studying law, his father having refused to subsidize a career in music. Out in Dakota Territory Theodore Roosevelt was busy punching cattle, bringing law and order to Dakota, hunting big game, and working on a book about his ranching and hunting, as well as on biographies of Thomas Hart Benton and Gouverneur Morris. No one would have predicted it then, but of the three men, Remington would be the first to achieve a national reputation in arts and letters.

Before leaving Kansas, Remington had written to Eva asking her to live with him in New York City while he tried, for a prescribed time, to become an illustrator; if he should fail, he would accept a job in business. The meteoric rise in Remington's fortune that took place at this point in his life astonished everyone. Within less than a year after his arrival in New York City with some crude Western sketches and no money, he had become a financially successful, nationally recognized illustrator.

Remington came to the city in 1885 at a moment opportune for what he had to offer. After the Civil War, there was a rapid growth in the popularity of illustrated magazines, especially the weeklies, with circulation made possible by a system of national railways and spur lines. Competent illustrators and engravers were much in demand for topics of current events, sports, adventure, invention, travel, and the like. Remington's sketches of men in action in the West were well suited to this market.

By the time Remington arrived in New York, Eva had come from Gloversville and set up housekeeping in an apartment in Brooklyn, subsidized by his Uncle Bill. By October Remington was making the rounds of magazine publishers. His interview with Henry Harper, head of the house of Harper, has become part of the myth of Remington as cowboy artist.

As told by Harper some years later, Remington came to the interview dressed in Western garb. He represented himself as a Yale football player who had gone west and become a cowboy on a ranch. Ranch life had failed and he was without money to get back to New York. Then he saw two gamblers cheating an Eastern drummer. He drew his pistol and rescued the man, then guarded him all night. In gratitude the drummer, who was also going back to New York, invited Remington to join him at his expense.

Even with a cowboy costume and some Western lingo, few men could have concocted the story Remington told and gotten away with it.

He had never been a cowboy; he had lost all his money in a saloon, not in a ranch; and his gunplay was limited to shooting up the night air as he galloped on the outskirts of Albany and Peabody. The dime-novel coincidence of the mutual New York destination should have alerted Henry Harper, but Remington had a talent for telling people what they wanted to hear.

Harper was beguiled by the story and by what he saw—a big, vigorous, self-confident cowboy, fresh from the Southwest. Harper and Brothers could use such a man. The interview established a personal relationship that lasted for years.

Harper bought two sketches, one of which, "The Apache War: Indian Scouts on Geronimo's Trail," appearing on the cover of *Harper's Weekly* (9 January 1886), was Remington's first professional illustration credited with his name. He was paid $150 for the two drawings, a respectable sum, but there were no immediate further assignments.

Subsidized again by Uncle Bill, Remington joined the Art Students League in March 1886, where fellow students included Ernest Thompson Seton and Charles Dana Gibson. There were outstanding instructors, and the students benefited from sharing their problems of technique. At the end of three months, however, Remington was ready to move on. Calling on Henry Harper again, he secured a plum assignment to go to the Southwest as an illustrator, covering the army's search for Geronimo, the Indian chief who had left the reservation and eluded capture.

It was on this commission that he met two men—the young Lieutenant Powhatan Clarke, a dashing cavalryman, and General Nelson Miles, the head of the expedition—both of whom became personal friends as well as sources of mutual benefit. Remington's illustrations and future articles praising the general and glorifying the activities of the lieutenant made popular heroes of both soldiers and at the same time promoted Remington's career as illustrator and writer.

Remington never did catch up with Geronimo. Once on the scene, he soon saw that the chase would be long and debilitating, with little chance of quick success. Without consultation, he changed the theme of his trip to "soldiering in the Southwest." Going to Tucson, he visited a Negro detachment of the 10th Cavalry, where he heard that a young officer had rescued a Negro soldier who had been shot through the legs. Dodging bullets, Lieutenant Clarke had dragged the corporal to safety. When Remington's dramatic *The Rescue of Corporal Scott* appeared as frontispiece in *Harper's Weekly* (21 August 1886), Clarke became a national hero, and General Miles was delighted to have Remington promote the story, giving the press and public something positive to say about the campaign.

Magazines other than *Harper's* now clamored for Remington's services, and his income soared. In 1886, his first year as a commercial artist, he earned $1,200, more than the average annual pay of teachers, ministers, or bureaucrats.

A letter to Powhatan Clarke expresses Remington's pleasure in his turn of fortune and also illustrates his lively style and his habitual errors in spelling and punctuation: "Say old top when you write me write sort of discriptive like. . . . I am hard at work—'getting there' so to speak. Thats a pretty good break for an ex-cowpuncher to come to New York with $30 and catch on in 'art.' Jesus it makes some of these old barnacles tired" (Samuels, 91–92). Remington, as usual, maintained the fiction that he had been a "cowpuncher," reluctant to admit he had engaged in sheepherding.

Once launched on a successful path, Remington threw himself into his work as eagerly as he had formerly dallied in office jobs. Not content with working in black and white, he honed his skills at watercolors, and in February 1887, he was rewarded when his submission was hung at the 20th Annual Exhibition of the American Water-Color Society and sold for the impressive sum of $85.

In April 1887 Remington obtained a commission from *Harper's* to visit the Canadian Northwest. His drawings of the Blackfoot Indians, the Crows, and the Canadian Mounties became regular full-page features in the magazine and added to his growing fame. As Peggy and Harold Samuels point out, Remington was not alone in his field. Dozens of professional artists had painted the American West before him. What set his work apart was its realism. He did not invest his Indians and cowboys with glamour but drew the frontier types as he saw them, his work "having the same freshness and incomparable native flavor that characterize Mark Twain's *Roughing It*" (Samuels, 94).

A major assignment came to Remington in the fall of 1887 when Theodore Roosevelt suggested him as illustrator for Roosevelt's *Ranch Life and the Hunting-Trail,* to be serialized in *Century Magazine* and published subsequently in book form. The commission called for 64 illustrations for the magazine and 19 more for the book. The two men met at this time, Remington taking an initial dislike to Roosevelt, whose manner he felt was condescending. Later, he modified his view, and the two became friendly, although Roosevelt's background of Harvard and "old family" tradition remained a barrier to closer ties.

By this date Remington was well known as an illustrator but had given little thought to himself as a potential author. His writing career began rather casually. His friend from Yale, Poultney Bigelow, now editor of *Outing* magazine, suggested that Remington write, as well as illustrate, an event from his Western experience. The result was a rollicking account of a hunt with his friends in his days in Kansas. Bigelow liked the lively style, and "Coursing Rabbits on the Plains" (*Outing,* May 1887) became Remington's first piece of professional writing.

The article was duly noted by *Century* editor Richard Watson Gilder, whom Remington had met while doing the Roosevelt assignment. In the spring of 1888, Gilder commissioned Remington to go out west to report on the "wild tribes," asking him to write as well as to illustrate the material. Remington modestly protested that he wasn't a writer, but Gilder cited the piece in *Outing,* and Remington set about the task with characteristic enthusiasm.

Before departing for the West, Remington wrote to his friend Lieutenant Powhatan Clarke, who was stationed at Fort Grant in Arizona, for help in finding his way into Indian Territory, but before Remington met with his first Indian tribe, he found himself on a scouting tour that would have dismayed many a lesser man. Arrived at Fort Grant, he learned that Clarke was scheduled for a two-week scout and that Remington was invited to go along and make his sketches. What neither of them knew was that Clarke, regarded as irresponsible by his commanding officer, was being punished by an intentionally rough assignment.

The episode is vividly described in Remington's article for *Century* "A Scout with the Buffalo-Soldiers" (April 1889). Accompanied by six black cavalrymen and Lieutenant Jim Watson, who was delegated to make the trip a torture, they were marched up the steep rise of the mountains, suffering from unbearable heat. They camped for many nights with a maximum of discomfort and were pressed to unholy speed on the return journey. Knowing he was overweight and out of condition, Remington feared he might fail but managed to make it through to the end. It was the first of many tests of strength and endurance that he set for himself in the ensuing years.

Although his commission from *Century* was to visit the Indian tribes, he had first changed the focus to an account of soldiering, as he had done in the *Harper's* assignment earlier. But, once recovered from the scouting episode, he set off to fulfill his obligation. From El Paso, where he was miserable with the heat and the mosquitoes, he found a wagon to take him to Fort Sill, the Comanche agency, and then on to Fort Reno to observe the Cheyennes, whom he came to admire above all other tribes. Two articles, "On the Indian Reservations" (*Century,* July 1889) and "Artist Wanderings among the Cheyennes" (*Century,* August 1889), show his first serious interest in Indians and their culture.

Meanwhile, before the other articles had appeared, Remington wrote a piece for Gilder on horses, a subject dear to his heart throughout his life. For many Americans, as well as for international admirers, his illustrations, paintings, and ultimately his sculptures of horses are among his most memorable works. "Horses of the Plains" (*Century,* January 1889) gives an account of the origin and development of the mustang and the bronco. Although the piece was edited more than once, Gilder seemed pleased with the result, for Eva wrote to Uncle Horace that "the Century people tell Fred he is quite a literary man."[2] By 1889 Remington's dual career as artist and writer was firmly established, and his work in both forms was in demand. Remington regarded himself primarily as an artist but was nevertheless pleased to have his writing admired and accepted.

In July 1888, when Remington arrived home in New York, he had the bizarre experience of reading in the press about his own suicide. The story ran in major newspapers throughout the country. The New York *Herald* headed its article "An Artist's Suicide. Frederick Remington, A Painter of Talent, Takes Morphine in Colorado." It was soon discovered that a Fred Remington, by coincidence an artist, had indeed taken a fatal dose of morphine at a hotel in Trinidad, Colorado, and the mystery was solved. The widespread publicity about the incident gave Remington flattering assurance of the extent of his fame at this date.

In a few short years, he had made enough money to regard himself as a rich man. As his income increased, he and Eva moved from Brooklyn to larger apartments uptown, and in December 1889 he purchased what he proudly called an "estate" on the "quality hill" of New Rochelle, a short train ride to midtown Manhattan. A fine brick house on three acres, with stables, trees, and gardens, he gave it the name "Endion," an Ojibwa word for "The place where I live." The couple never had the children they had hoped for—Eva suffered from chronic disease of the ovaries—but they remained devoted and affectionate. He called her the Kid, and she referred to him as her big boy, tolerating his drinking bouts with his pals and trying in vain to curb his excess weight.

Remington now decided he could afford to devote more time to serious art. Early in 1889 he had submitted a large oil, *Last Lull in the Fight,* to the American jury for the Paris International Exposition and had been delighted to win a second-place medal. His commission to illustrate Henry Wadsworth Longfellow's *Hiawatha* for *Harper's Monthly* combined both painting and sketches, requiring 22 paintings to be used as full-page plates. As his skill increased, he began exhibiting his paintings, and in June 1891 he was elected an Associate of the National Academy of Design. To his disappointment, he never achieved the status of Academician. The establishment continued to regard him as a "commercial" artist, failing to recognize the achievements of his final years.

Ever since his contacts with the cavalry soldiers in the West, Remington had been keen on the excitement of the warfare with the Indians. He had accompanied General Miles on a peace expedition, but late in 1890, when the Sioux leader Sitting Bull was killed by a detail of troops, the uprising burst into full-scale war, ending in the tragedy of the battle of Wounded Knee. On 29 December, more than 150 Indian men, women, and children were slaughtered, in what was to be the end of the Indian wars. Remington had eagerly sought a commission from *Harper's* to cover the action and was close to the Pine Ridge Agency at the time. He was not there at the battle itself, however, but was near enough to hear soldiers talk about it afterward and to have his only actual encounter with hostile Indians. Riding toward the agency, where he hoped to get close to the fighting, he and his party encountered a group of painted Sioux. After a few terrifying moments, five armed settlers rode up by chance, and Remington's party turned and galloped back to the army base (Samuels, 150).

At this date Remington saw war as he wanted it to be: a rigorous cavalry pursuit alleviated with intervals of cheerful camaraderie, the Indian as heroic adversary, and stoic soldiers going to battle. He did not see the butchery of the battle itself; rather, like many of his contemporaries, he saw war as a noble pursuit.

When he had the chance to go abroad with Poultney Bigelow in 1892, he was strongly attracted by Bigelow's hint that there might soon be war between Germany and Russia. The war didn't take place, but they met in Berlin with the kaiser and went on to St. Petersburg, where Bigelow, unknown to Remington, gathered information about Russian troop activity on behalf of the kaiser. The Russians were suspicious and promptly deported them. Remington went on to France, where he saw works of Monet, whom he came to appreciate more fully at a later date. In London, he was dazzled by Buffalo Bill Cody's Wild West Show. On the whole, however, he never cared for foreign travel, nor for that matter for foreigners.

In the summer of 1893, a significant friendship began when Remington met Owen Wister by chance while traveling in the Yellowstone. Wister's first Western stories had recently been published by *Harper's*, and he was impressed at meeting the famous artist and illustrator. The two men were physical contrasts. As Wister wrote to his mother: "I am a thin and despondent man . . . but Remington weighs about 240 pounds and is a huge rollicking animal" (Samuels, 195).

Wister, a year older than Remington, came from a distinguished family in Philadelphia. After Harvard, where he was an excellent scholar, he studied music in Paris for a year until his father insisted he return and study law. Because of ill health, he had spent time in Wyoming, where he developed a passion for the West that became the major theme of his writing career.

From their first meeting, a working collaboration began. Remington illustrated many of Wister's works, gave him copious details on Western lore, and was the driving force behind Wister's well-known 1895 essay "The Evolution of the Cow-Puncher."

Wister had known Theodore Roosevelt at Harvard, and with his meeting Remington, the triumvirate was complete: the three men who, through prose, fiction, and art, created the popular vision of the American West.

In the year 1895 Remington was elated when Harper brought out *Pony Tracks*, an anthology of 15 of his pieces previously published in its magazines. The dedication is "to the fellows who rode the ponies that made the tracks," and the book brought Remington enormous pride. As the author of a book, he could now regard himself as a real "literary" man. The book was well reviewed, and Harper followed it with similar collections: *Crooked Trails* (1898), *Stories of Peace and War* (1899), *Men with the Bark On* (1900).

The same year, 1895, brought a dramatic new direction to Remington as artist. His friend Augustus Thomas suggested that with his eye for shapes, Remington ought to be a sculptor. When Thomas's friend, the sculptor Frederick W. Ruckstall, came to New Rochelle to model an equestrian statue, Remington watched in fascination as the clay took shape and eagerly tried his hand at the new medium with remarkable success. His first bronze, *The Bronco Buster*, was cast by the Henry-Bonnard foundry in October 1895 and met with much praise. Elated, he wrote to Bigelow, who was in Europe at the time, "When you Europeans get your two eyes on my bronze you will say: 'Ah, there—America has got a winner.' Its the biggest business I ever did and if some of these rich sinners over here will cough up and buy a couple of dozen I will go into the mud business" (Samuels, 228). For all his flippancy, Remington took his sculpting seriously, writing to Wister that his paintings might fade but he believed he might "endure in bronze"—an accurate prophecy, for bronzes on Western subjects are among the major foundations of his lasting reputation today.

By 1895 Remington's desire to see a "real war" began to look like a possibility. As the frontier era of American history drew to a close, attention turned to foreign matters. In Cuba, active insurrection was heating up under Spanish rule. Stories of atrocities incited popular protest in the press, spurred by the "yellow" journalism of William Randolph Hearst's *New York Journal* and its rival, the *New York World*. Remington was delighted when Hearst commissioned him, along with the journalist Richard Harding Davis, to cover the situation in Cuba in December 1896. Although the two men never reached the insurgents, they spent some time in Havana, becoming the source for a notorious journalistic legend. When Remington informed Hearst that all was quiet and there was no war, Hearst reputedly wired back, "You furnish the pictures and I'll furnish the war." Whatever the causes of the war, there is little doubt that reports and pictures of deplorable conditions in Cuba contributed to both popular and official willingness to become involved. On 15 February 1898, the sinking of the battleship *Maine* in Havana harbor pushed President McKinley to action, although it was not until 21 April that war was officially declared.

When U.S. troops first landed at Daiquirí on 22 June 1898, they met with no resistance, as the Spanish, to Remington's disappointment, pulled back toward the town of Santiago. The invasion was a "lark," as from a hilltop he watched the troops move forward. On the first day, he joined up with his old friends of the now-unhorsed cavalry and enjoyed an elegant picnic lunch as the guest of General Young. During the night, Theodore Roosevelt had his first taste of fame as a hero when he and his Rough Riders were involved in a skirmish, and Remington missed it. Disgruntled, he and another correspondent, the novelist John Fox, decided to stay close to the front, abandoning the protection of the general's tents and sleeping in the open, a disastrous decision for a man who was vastly overweight and in poor physical condition. Within a few days, he fell ill, had little to eat and less to drink, and by 30 June, debilitated and exhausted, he was 1,000 yards in the rear when Roosevelt and his Riders made their historic charge on San Juan Hill. He had dodged enough bullets and shrapnel to satisfy any urge for danger or any need to test his own courage, but he had not become the dashing war hero he had revered in memories of his father.

Glorious as were the cheers of victory, it was the sights at a field hospital and the horrors at the rear of the battle that haunted him. Modern warfare was nothing like his ideal of mounted cavalry making forays in the Indian wars. He saw instead "a modern war against an adversary who was seldom seen, with no finesse involved at all in a conflict where men on foot accept the ultimate brutalization to mount a primitive charge up a fortified hill" (Samuels, 282). Physically and emotionally spent, he made his way out of Cuba and home to Endion to recuperate, his Cuban experience ultimately immortalized by his illustrations and paintings of the event.

In 1900 Remington and Eva acquired a summer place called Ingleneuk, a small island on the St. Lawrence River not far from his childhood home in Ogdensburg. Supplies were brought in by boat to the remodeled cottage and studio, where he painted and wrote but also relaxed with canoeing, swimming, and fishing. This was his haven from the pressures of city life, and he loved it.

As his confidence as a writer grew, Remington ventured into fiction. "The Great Medicine-Horse: An Indian Myth of the Thunder" (*Harper's Monthly*, September 1897) introduces Sun-Down Leflare, a half-breed Indian based loosely on a character he had met many years earlier. Raised as a Roman Catholic, Sun-Down amusingly presents the contrast between his native Indian tradition and the teachings of the white man. Four more Sun-Down stories followed, and the five were collected by Harper in 1899. *Sun-Down Leflare* met with less success than other Remington anthologies, perhaps because readers were distracted with the events of the war.

Two historical inventions, "Joshua Goodenough's Old Letter" and "Massai's Crooked Trail," were well received, the latter drawing gratifying praise from Theodore Roosevelt, who wrote, "Are you aware . . . you come closer to the real thing with the pen than any other man in the western business?" (*CW*, 614).

Edging his way toward longer fiction, Remington now wrote his first novel, *The Way of an Indian*, depicting the life of a Cheyenne from boyhood to chief of his tribe, his death signaling the end of a proud culture, defeated by the advent of the white man. The Indian's point of view is given without sentimentality, neither the noble savage nor the victim, merely a member of a radically different tradition.

The publication of the novel met with a curious delay. The Samuels provide evidence that the writing was completed by the summer of 1900, but the novel was not published until some years later (Samuels, 297). Intended as a serial for a magazine William Randolph Hearst was about to launch, the manuscript and illustrations languished until Hearst purchased the *Cosmopolitan* in 1905, and *The Way of an Indian* finally appeared in five installments from November 1905 to March 1906 and in book form in that year.

Meanwhile, Remington had written *John Ermine of the Yellowstone,* the novel he regarded as his ultimate literary achievement. Its publication in November 1902 marked essentially the end of Remington's writing life. The story of a white boy raised by Indians but taught white man's ways by an old hermit, it is a fine study of the inevitable tragedy that confronts the man when he attempts to bridge the gap between the two cultures. The novel was well reviewed, sold well, and was dramatized on the New York stage the following year. Owen Wister's *The Virginian,* which had appeared earlier in the same year, had become a runaway best-seller. Remington felt, with some justice, that the formulaic happy ending of Wister's work weakened its impact, and that his own ending was truer to reality. Remington was pleased with his accomplishment but ready to give up writing and devote himself to serious painting.

After 1902 Remington also began to withdraw from the illustrating that had been so lucrative. He no longer needed to earn money, and for the remaining seven years of his life, he returned to the pursuit of fine art that he had rejected in his student days at Yale and had to some extent neglected in the interim. His skill in color advanced, and his oils began to take on the influence of the Impressionists, while retaining his own unique treatment of his subjects. A series of "Nocturnes" showed exceptional skill in night scenes. The Samuels express the opinion, shared by many art critics, that Remington was on the way to becoming "one of America's most powerful fine artists. The limit to what he might have been was curtailed only by his early death at a time when he could have had twenty years of growth ahead of him" (x).

Remington's work in bronze culminated in 1908 in the spectacular 12-foot statue *The Cowboy,* which stands on the edge of a cliff in Fairmont Park in Philadelphia.

In 1908 Remington put both Endion and Ingleneuk up for sale and launched the building of an enormous mansion in Ridgefield, Connecticut, where he looked forward to association with the group of artists there. The couple moved into their new home in May 1909 but had only a few months to enjoy its luxuries. A few days before Christmas, Remington fell ill with severe abdominal pain. On the 23rd, the doctors performed an appendectomy, but the appendix had burst and peritonitis had set in. He slipped into a coma and died the morning of 26 December 1909, at the age of 48.

Chapter Two
Soldiering in the West

In the spring of 1905, *Collier's* magazine published a "Remington" issue, devoted to the now-famous artist and writer. In a short piece, Remington himself reflects on an incident some 24 years earlier that stirred him to record the passing of the West.

On a night in Montana in 1881, at the age of 19, he had come across the campfire of an old man who had run freight wagons on westward journeys. Remington had come west with "schoolboy enthusiasm," he wrote, sweating along the trail of Lewis and Clark and others, but gradually he perceived that times had changed. Now, the old freighter, sharing his bacon and coffee with Remington over the campfire, told his story. He had been born in New York and gone west to Iowa. Then, during his long life, he had followed the receding frontiers, always moving further westward. Now, he said, there is no more West. Soon the railroad would come and a poor man couldn't make a living at all. Looking at the old man, Remington reflects:

> There he was . . . sleeping in a blanket on the ground . . . eating . . . out of his frying-pan, wearing a cotton shirt open at the throat, and hunting his horses through the bleak hills before daylight; and all for enough money for 'harness' and 'wagon grease.' I knew the railroad was coming—I saw men already swarming into the land. . . . I knew the wild riders and the vacant land were about to vanish forever. . . . Without knowing exactly how to do it, I began to try to record some facts around me, and the more I looked the more the panorama unfolded. (*CW,* 550–51)

The scene is vivid, as if Remington were making notes for a painting: two men at a campfire, a freight wagon, horses in a dim background, and perhaps in the sunset sky some hint in cloud and shadow of the panorama of westering frontiersmen, somewhat like the cavalcade of ancestors in his illustration for Owen Wister's "Evolution of the Cow-Puncher" in *Harper's Monthly* of September 1895. The scene is also archetypal. The old freighter is the Vanishing American, a brother to Cooper's Natty Bumppo in *The Prairie,* reduced to trapping in the Far

West, or to the grandfather in Steinbeck's *Red Pony,* whose westering has come to its end at the California coast. One can see the popular image of a lone Indian on a bare-ribbed horse that, along with a decorated print of the poem "Out Where the West Begins," once hung in every ranchhouse parlor. Finally, there is in the incident the mythic moment when the traveler hears the call to pen or paint or preach the word.

By 1905, when Remington wrote this passage in *Collier's,* the lamentation for the passing of the heroic West had become a commonplace. In his "Note to the Reader" in *The Virginian* (1902), Owen Wister wrote that the Wyoming of his romance was "a vanished world" and his "horseman of the plains would never come again." Wister, too, had had his nocturnal experience. In 1930 he recalled an evening in the fall of 1891, shortly after he had returned from a Wyoming trip, when, after oysters and coffee and over some excellent claret at his Philadelphia club, he resolved to save "the sage-brush for American literature before . . . it went the way of everything."[1] He thereupon retired to the club library, and by midnight he had completed a good portion of "Hank's Woman," his first Western story.

Remington's interest in soldiers in the West began in 1886 when Henry Harper sent him on assignment to illustrate the army's pursuit of Geronimo under General Nelson Miles. He never caught up with Geronimo, but he formed two important friendships on this assignment, the one with General Miles himself, the other with Lieutenant Powhatan Clarke, both of whom became rich sources of information about military life and Indian battles.

Two years later, Richard Watson Gilder, editor of *Century* magazine, commissioned Remington to go out west and report on the "wild tribes," assigning him to do the writing as well as the illustrations. Although this was a prestigious assignment, in a monthly rather than a weekly journal, Remington, with brash self-confidence, changed the focus from wild Indians to the U.S. Cavalry without consulting his editor. Gilder was evidently pleased with the result, however, and a narrative essay, "A Scout with the Buffalo Soldiers," appeared in the April 1889 issue of *Century,* recounting the episode of the preceding year.

The 10th Cavalry of the regular army, designated as "Colored," had interested Remington from the time, two years earlier, when he had enjoyed meeting with a detachment of black soldiers led by Lieutenant Powhatan Clarke. Called "Buffalo Soldiers" by the Indians, the 10th had proudly adopted the title and made a buffalo the central design in the regimental crest.

In June 1888, Remington joined Lieutenant Clarke at Fort Grant, an outpost near the juncture of the Gila and the San Pedro rivers in southeastern Arizona. Along with six black cavalrymen of a company of the 10th, Remington and Clarke started on a 12-day "scout," a tour from Fort Grant to the San Carlos Agency and back. The march was routed over rough, mountainous country, and Remington, overweight and out of condition, feared he might not see it through.

In the article, Remington presents himself as a man from New York, going along as an observer. Some events are described with the self-deprecatory humor that became a Remington trademark. In one illustration of troops descending a steep mountain trail, the New Yorker is seen as a stout man picking his way in the rear. The tone turns serious, however, when he describes the hardships of soldiering and the admirable behavior of the black troopers.

In the outbound portion of the scouting tour, the heat and dust, the rocky trails and steep mountains, and the jolting, stumbling, and straining are painful and exhausting, but there is joking along the way and socializing at stops. At Fort Thomas they refresh themselves for the return, but the march back is torture. They go over the highest ridges at great speed, make dry camp between distant water holes, almost lose a man and horse when a ledge gives way, while two others nearly sink in quicksand. The New Yorker survives the ordeal, but arrives back at Fort Grant with floundering movements and sunburned face, "firm in the conviction that soldiers, like other men, find more hard work than glory in their calling" (CW, 30). Remington was elated at his own success and never knew that the trip had been designed to test the endurance of both Clarke and the "man from New York" (Samuels, 108).

The article is notable for the glowing account Remington gives of the Negro soldiers. He observes that in the face of hardship, the black troopers, rather than complaining, occupied themselves "in joking and in merriment," and he goes on to observe of Negro troops in general that they are charming men with whom to serve.

> Officers have often confessed to me that when they . . . are troubled with a depression of spirits, they have only to go about the campfires of the negro soldier in order to be amused and cheered by the clever absurdities of the men. . . . As to their bravery, I am often asked, "Will they fight?" That is easily answered. They have fought many, many times. The old sergeant sitting near me . . . once deliberately walked over a Cheyenne rifle pit and killed his man. One little fellow near him once took charge

of a lot of stampeded cavalry horses when Apache bullets were flying loose. . . . The little episodes prove the sometimes doubted self-reliance of the negro. (*CW,* 25)

Remington's views on race and ethnicity were complex. He was a man of his time, often making derogatory remarks about other races, sharing the widely held view that the country founded by Anglo-Saxons was being corrupted by foreign immigration. Yet in his personal contact with black soldiers, with Mexican cowboys, or with Indians who were not "savage," he expresses in writing and illustrations his admiration for these people, against the current of popular prejudice.

Remington's admiration for model men of arms recurs throughout his writing. He glories in regular companies of seasoned cavalrymen armed with rifle and six-shooter, supplied by packmule. He admires, and illustrates, hard-riding young field officers and energetic generals operating in a hostile land with only scattered outposts for supply and recuperation.

In "Two Gallant Young Cavalrymen" (*Harper's Weekly,* 22 March 1890), a small band of Apaches is captured by a company of black troopers and Indian scouts led by Lieutenants Powhatan Clarke and James Watson. Both officers are Remington's ideal of "young, hardy, enterprising, and, above all, intelligent" cavalrymen (*CW,* 49). The article also praises General Miles, known for his outstanding service in the West. Miles is portrayed as an enterprising military strategist, shrewd and experienced in Indian warfare.

The personal friendship between Miles and Remington proved mutually beneficial. Remington could publicize Miles, and Miles could provide Remington an entry to the army for firsthand observations. Socially they were compatible. Both enjoyed hunting, riding, good food, and fine clothing, and Remington may well have found in Miles a surrogate for his father, who had died before Frederic's 21st birthday.

Later that year, Miles headed the Cheyenne Indian Commission, which was to determine whether to move the Northern Cheyenne from their reservation in Montana. At Miles's invitation, Remington accompanied the commission as correspondent for *Harper's Weekly.* In the issue of 6 December 1890, two articles from the Montana assignment appeared.

In the first of these, "Chasing a Major-General," Miles is Remington's man of action, the dashing combat officer, a warrior respected by warriors, and a good negotiator as well. "The commission had talked to a ring of drowsy old chiefs, and the general had reminded them that he

ON THE SOUTHERN PLAINS, OIL ON CANVAS BY FREDERIC REMINGTON
(1907)
Courtesy the Metropolitan Museum of Art, Gift of Several Gentlemen, 1911.

had thrashed them once, and was perfectly willing to do it again if they
did not keep in the middle of the big road" (*CW,* 54).

This article shows an advance in the literary quality of Remington's
writing. It was the earliest piece to be included in the *Harper's* anthology
Pony Tracks (1895) and was praised by critic Royal Cortissoz for its
"directness and close-packed simplicity" (Samuels, 145).

There was no hint of any trouble brewing in "Chasing a Major-
General." The company rode through a peaceful valley of subdued Indians. However, the second Remington piece in the issue, "The Art of War
and Newspaper Men," notes a present threat. The army had to censor
news of preparations and troop movements because many Indians in
recent years had learned to read. Hence Oglalas and the Sitting Bull
people might go scampering over the plains and make alliance with the
Cheyennes before General Miles could organize his show of force. The
article echoed the sort of bombast and war-scare that had been appearing in newspapers nationally. Remington put the problem in simple
terms: "I realize that before this matter is printed, the biggest Indian
war since 1758 will be in progress, or that the display of military force
will have accomplished its object, and the trouble gone" (*CW,* 58). On
29 December 1890, the massacre at Wounded Knee gave the answer.

Meanwhile, General Miles was less concerned with a grand alliance of Cheyennes and Sioux than with the state of anarchy on the reservations of four Sioux tribes, where armed Indians were withdrawing to a stronghold and old chiefs were reasserting authority. As Miles worked to reestablish order, the war interest began to wane. Then on 15 December Sitting Bull, who had become something of a national hero, was killed in a fight with Indian policemen, and the situation became explosive.

On 17 December Miles took over direct command of field operations. Remington got permission to join the general's staff and negotiated with *Harper's Weekly* to do war drawings at $100 per page. After a week with Miles at Rapid City, Remington elected to join his friend Lieutenant Edward Casey and his Fort Keogh Cheyenne Scout Corps, hoping he might see some action firsthand. He spent Christmas with soldiers cheerfully making the best they could of poor whisky, a cold tent, and scant tobacco, described, a year later, in "A Merry Christmas in a Sibley Tepee" (*Harper's Weekly*, 5 December 1891).

After Christmas they moved to a camp on the Cheyenne River about 30 miles from the Pine Ridge Agency, with orders to avoid battle if possible. On 27 December the Sioux at the stronghold near Lieutenant Casey's encampment began to move hesitantly back toward Pine Ridge Agency. Then on 29 December, 20 miles east of the agency, came Wounded Knee. More than 150 Indian men, women, and children and 25 officers and men were killed, and many on both sides were wounded.

Unaware of this event, Remington decided to go to the Pine Ridge Agency, where most of the war reporters were assembled. On the way, he faced his only encounter with hostile Indians when his party encountered a group of painted Sioux and managed to escape back to their camp.

Remington had not been at the last battle of the Indian war, but he was close enough to hear firsthand reports from soldiers who were. "The Sioux Outbreak in South Dakota" (*Harper's Weekly*, 27 January 1891) was Remington's contribution to the literature of Wounded Knee. He begins with a lighthearted explanation of how he missed the battle itself, then moves to what he heard. He reconstructs the dialogue of men in the tepees and hospital tents of the Seventh Cavalry. It is the talk of soldiers, men who speak with brevity of their deeds and their wounds. There is the soldier's respect for the fighting quality of the Indian warrior, the officer's respect for the fighting quality of the private, the admiration for the competence of the artillery men, the silence that falls at the mention of the death of a captain, the wounded soldier who is going to reenlist "to get square with these Injuns" (*CW,* 69). The incident is seen as heroic on both sides, where brave and skillful soldiers fought against brave and skillful warriors, misled by false prophets.

By 5 January Remington was on the train back to New York, where he was grieved to hear the news that Lieutenant Casey had been killed on a peace mission to a Sioux village. "Lieutenant Casey's Last Scout: On the Hostile Flanks with the Chis-Chish-Chash" (*Harper's Weekly,* 31 January 1891) is Remington's tribute to the young officer and his untimely death.[2] He describes the rigors of his scouting journey with Casey in the bitter cold. After the battle, Casey had gone to a Sioux tent to seek a peace accord and had been shot by the enemy. Remington laments the loss of this fine young officer, "beloved by his comrades, respected by his generals and by the Secretary of War" (*CW,* 77).

At this date, Remington saw war as he wanted war to be: a rigorous cavalry pursuit, alleviated with intervals of cheerful camaraderie; the Indian as both friend and foe; and stoic soldiers going to battle. If he had witnessed the melee at Wounded Knee or seen the battlefield with the frozen corpses of men, women, and children, he might have taken a different view. Later, in Cuba, he was to see the ugly realities of war.

On 16 January 1892, *Harper's Weekly* carried a curious article, "The Galloping Sixth." The title and the illustrations indicate an account of a unit in the field, but the article was, in fact, a personal attack on Colonel Eugene A. Carr, whose camp Remington had visited just before joining Lieutenant Casey's scouts. The colonel, who did not meet Remington's picture of the dashing cavalryman, is caricatured as a "bacon and forage" man to whom "fighting is a mere detail" (*CW,* 91). The article was printed simultaneously in the *Army and Navy Journal* and provoked a tempest of letter writing, with some army men defending Carr and others defending Remington as a friend of the army.

Whether Remington wrote of the West as current event or as history, he regarded the regular army as the force that tamed the frontier. One exception was his admiration for the Texas Rangers. In "How the Law Got into the Chaparral" (*Harper's Monthly,* December 1896), Remington recounts stories told him by three old Rangers in the San Antonio Club, occasionally interspersing his own assessments. The dialogue is sometimes gritty, sometimes understated, always lively. Bits of Texas lore appear: the Rangers' early use of the Colt six-shooter and later, the Gatling gun, and the decimation of the Meir expedition, where each man's death was determined by drawing a black bean, illustrated by a drawing of an 1838 Colt revolver and a painting of *Prisoners Drawing*

Their Beans. The tales provide a brief history of the Rangers, formed in the 1830s to fight Mexicans and Commanches and reorganized in 1876 to "carry the law into the chaparral," a land infested with border bandits, Mexican and Texan cattle thieves, and unruly settlers. They began essentially as an army fighting large bands of Mexicans and Commanches and operating in companies of more than a hundred men, sometimes augmented by a company of Indian scouts.

What is remarkable about Remington's assessment is his obvious approval of the power the Rangers were given and assumed. The captains had absolute authority to enlist and to discharge. At times, the Rangers were "judge, jury and executioner" (*CW,* 246), even to the extent of ignoring disreputable sheriffs and international boundaries. Remington sees the Rangers as men of good character, fine riders and dead shots, filled with the spirit of adventure and a "perfect willingness to die" (*CW,* 246). They took no prisoners in battle and did not bother to "count Mexicans" in tallying their kill.

By the end of 1890, Remington had established himself as author, illustrator, and friend of the army that had fought the Indians. After Wounded Knee, he acknowledged the value of the training, on the European model, of the Eastern army, with its advances in weaponry and uniforms, but his heart was with the seasoned soldiers out West who knew there was more hard work than glory in soldiering. Between 1891 and 1902 he wrote a number of pieces, some fact, some fiction, recalling incidents and exploits of the past and keeping readers posted on how the heroes of those days were faring in the present.

"Training Cavalry Horses to Jump Obstacles" (*Harper's Weekly,* 9 September 1891) discusses a series of experiments conducted by Lieutenants Clark and Smith of the 10th Cavalry. Horses were being taught to jump over natural obstacles rather than over the artificial hurdles of the Eastern riding halls where the "high school" of horsemanship was being conducted. He makes some cogent remarks on the training and conditioning of horses and illustrates the experiments with a montage of horses jumping over, balking at, or falling over piles of logs and a dead steer. In this essay and throughout his military accounts, Remington's cavalryman is a hard rider, but he also rides a well-kept horse.

In "The Advance-Guard, or the Military Sacrifice" (*Harper's Weekly,* 31 January 1891), Remington pays tribute to the workaday courage of the common soldier in the Indian wars. He outlines the need for the advance guard—the "vidette," the "point man"—and cites his personal recognition of the peril faced by these men. "I have experienced myself the feeling of going up a narrow trail to a mesa which was supposed to harbor hundreds of Sioux" (*CW,* 109). He quotes from the 1757 diary of Major Robert Rogers, a great Indian fighter, who advises on the necessity of using advance guards in military action, citing the principle that it is better to sacrifice one or two men than a dozen, or possibly all of a command.

The article closes with an elegy for the point man who rides up the canyons with his life on his sleeve: "He hears a report, feels a shock, reels in his saddle, while his stricken horse plunges under him, and then the dull brain reels and faints; but the captain in command knows that the ground in front is occupied, and takes measure in accordance" (*CW,* 110). An illustration shows the sacrifice, as a trooper reels in the saddle, his horse faltering, and the other point man races back down the canyon to the distant command. The death of the advance guard is an instance of a Remington theme: the untimely, and often lonely, death of the frontier hero. That soldier may have ridden out alone a dozen times; this time a bullet from somewhere struck him.

In September 1896 Remington met with old friends from the Geronimo days: Lieutenant Carter Johnson and troops of the 10th Cavalry, now stationed at Fort Assiniboine in northwest Montana. Remington rode out on maneuvers with a Negro infantry command. The high point of the adventure was an unauthorized but exhilarating cavalry charge that Johnson led against the infantry camp, simply as a lark. The maneuvers provided the material for Remington's first piece for *Cosmopolitan* magazine, "Vagabonding with the Tenth Horse" (February 1897). He took the opportunity to praise again the quality of the Negro soldier. As for the charge, it was "magnificent," but an infantryman observed that in a real assault the cavalry would have been shot down before they reached the camp.

Remington had met Johnson when he was a guest of Lieutenant Powhatan Clarke at Fort Grant, and just as "A Scout with the Buffalo Soldiers" in 1889 was followed by an essay in praise of the gallant Clarke, so "Vagabonding with the Tenth Horse" was followed by one in praise of Johnson. "A Sergeant of the Orphan Troop" (*Harper's Monthly,* August 1897) describes events that occurred some 18 years earlier, showing Johnson as gallant but also compassionate. In January 1879, near Fort Robinson, Nebraska, Johnson was the sergeant of a Third Cavalry troop without its own field officer, hence the "orphan" troop. The account tells of two events. In the first, Johnson, without official authorization, takes his men to help some troopers who have corralled a group of Cheyennes. Johnson and another trooper volunteer to scout ahead. They wipe out an ambush, Johnson's troop advances, the Indians surrender, and the troop returns to the fort in high spirits, with Sergeant Johnson carrying an Indian baby in his arms.

In contrast, the second episode describes what was perhaps the bloodiest incident in the campaign to force the Northern Cheyennes onto a reservation in Indian Territory. Johnson and his troops were ordered to ride out again to pursue and capture the chief Dull Knife and some 120 Northern Cheyennes. For 10 days the cavalry, accompanied by an artillery unit, follow the Dull Knife trail, pursuing fleeing Indians, who slip out of entrapments. Cold, hungry, frustrated cavalrymen pursue starving, freezing Indians until the "Spartan band" of Cheyennes turns and makes its last stand. Enraged soldiers and suicidal Indian men and women fight with pistols, knives, and clubbed rifles, with Johnson fighting as savagely as anyone, until abruptly he stops, shouts that he will do no more, kicks the gun out of a soldier's hand, and declares, "This fight is over" (*CW,* 262).[3]

How much of the account is fact and how much fiction is debatable. What is important is that six years after Wounded Knee, desperate Indians are described as "Spartans," and cavalrymen are seen as enraged killers of men, women, and children. This is the only piece Remington wrote that describes in detail an actual battle of the Indian wars, and it poses the question of when battle becomes slaughter, in the very year that Remington was waiting impatiently for a "real" war in Cuba that might give the U.S. Cavalry the chance to do its soldiers' work.

By this date, Remington had developed considerable confidence in himself as a writer, not merely as a journalist. In "Joshua Goodenough's Old Letter" (*Harper's Monthly,* November 1897), he gives an excellent fictional creation of a letter from a soldier in the French and Indian War a century earlier. Dated "Albany 1798," Joshua writes to his son, recounting his experiences with Captain Rogers's irregulars. Remington deftly captures the unsentimental prose of the soldier's dogged loyalty and unheralded courage as he describes a series of encounters with the enemy. The piece was reprinted in paper wraps in 1897, titled *A Rogers Ranger in the French and Indian War, 1757–1759,* and was included in two *Harper's* anthologies, *Crooked Trails* (1898) and *Stories of Peace and War* (1899).

Another finely written piece, "Massai's Crooked Trail" (*Harper's Monthly,* January 1898), drew praise from Theodore Roosevelt, among others. Based upon the elusive Apache who had escaped when Geronimo was captured, Massai had returned to Arizona, making phantom appearances and magically evading capture, raping and murdering as he traveled. In a letter to Remington, Roosevelt wrote: "Are you aware, O sea-going plainsman, that aside from what you do with the pencil, you come closer to the real thing with the pen than any other man in the western business?" (Samuels, 258).

In two articles in the following year, Remington deals with contrasting modes of training for cavalry. "The Essentials at Fort Adobe" (*Harper's Monthly*, April 1898) praises the field training in the West, where "active, hard-riding, straight-shooting, open-order men are doing real work" (*CW*, 289). In "The Training of Cavalry" (*Harper's Weekly*, 2 April 1898), he describes the trainees at Fort Meyer, Virginia, where troops of the Sixth Cavalry (the "Galloping Sixth") were instructed in the "new system of horse-training and Cossack-riding, at which they did better than any circus he had seen" (*CW*, 292). While acknowledging the skill of the Eastern school, Remington views the Western cavalry as superior in skill and practical experience. Both groups, he points out, require extensive training, and he ends with a warning to "those blatant patriots" (*CW*, 294) who fail to appreciate the time needed to train men for the cavalry, and who naively believe that, in the event of war, a vast number of untrained volunteers could meet the challenge.

"An Interesting Detail" (*Harper's Weekly*, 8 January 1898) is another example of recalling a past exploit of a cavalry officer. Lieutenant Guy H. Preston of the Ninth Cavalry, currently in charge of sending pack trains to Alaska, was such a hero. In 1890, then with the Seventh Cavalry, he was the messenger who carried the news of the fight at Wounded Knee to Pine Ridge, riding through "a country full of Indians" (*CW*, 283). The adventure of "carrying the message" recalls such popular works as Longfellow's "Paul Revere's Ride" and Browning's "How They Brought the Good News from Ghent to Aix."

On 15 February 1898 the battleship *Maine* blew up in Havana harbor and Remington saw firsthand the brutal realities of a "real" war. (See chapter 6, "The Martial Spirit.")

After the Cuba experience, Remington turned back to "that old cleaning up of the West," as he put it in a letter to Owen Wister in September 1899.[4] Now, however, his focus becomes more clearly historical. He writes of incidents outside his personal experience and before his own time there. The old-timer becomes a persistent figure in his narratives, and like the old Cheyenne chiefs in Montana, the old soldier is the last of his kind. Remington's tone becomes more sober and his work more complex and ambiguous. He is, in effect, reexamining his treatment of the West.

"When a Document Is Official" (*Harper's Monthly,* September 1899) is a short story set at Fort Adobe in the winter of a year when "Mr. Sitting-Bull" and "Mr. Crazy-Horse" are abroad in the land. A Sergeant Burling has been told that his officer's commission, for which he had worked nine grueling years, has just been signed. He is about to celebrate with a good drink when the colonel asks him to deliver an order to an officer in the field. The theme is "carrying the message," as in "An Interesting Detail," but the circumstance here is a tragic irony. Instead of the straightforward adventure tale of Lieutenant Preston or of a literary figure like Paul Revere, the messenger never gets through, and the importance of the message itself is not known. We know only that the colonel says it is important. A buffalo hunter to whom it would have no real value attempts to steal it. Burling is killed by Indians who never know of the document. Soldierly pride in his new commission leads to Burling's death.

The ironies in the story represent Remington's new approach to his theme. He seems to be saying that courage, experience, devotion to duty, and a fast horse do not guarantee success. The last word is given to an old Indian who, speaking of "white man's medicine," says, "It make dam fool of soldiers lots of time I know 'bout." (*CW,* 393)

"How Stilwell Sold Out" (*Collier's,* 16 December 1899) is another account of "carrying the message." It is based upon the Battle of Beecher's Island, September 1868, where 50 scouts, commanded by Major George Forsyth, fortified themselves on an island in a fork of the Republican River and stood off several hundred Sioux and Cheyenne Dog Soldiers for a week until they were relieved by troops from Fort Wallace. Although the battle was of comparatively little military significance, it soon became a part of the folklore of the Indian wars and later a mythic scene in Western movies. Jack Stilwell and an old Rocky Mountain French trapper named Trudeau, disguised as Indians, walked more than 100 miles to the fort for help.

The article differs from other Remington tales of Indian wars heroism in that the two heroes are not regular army soldiers. Major Forsyth's scouts were frontiersmen enlisted to guard the railroad west from Fort Wallace. Stilwell was a professional hunter, Trudeau a trapper. The account of the long trek is a story of the devices of frontier survival and the loyalty of frontier companions. What gives the piece much of its vitality is the characterization of the two men. Trudeau is an old French

Northwester in greasy buckskins, aged beyond his years by hard living and hard drinking. Stilwell is a mere boy but already with a reputation as an excellent horseman and a crack shot. They are the archetypal pairing of veteran wisdom and youthful talent.

The title of the piece is ironic. Stilwell and Trudeau vow they will sell themselves dearly if they are stopped by Indians. Since the mission succeeds, the last sentence reads, "So Jack Stilwell never 'sold out' after all" (*CW*, 400).

Two pieces of this period take soldiers to the Philippines. "They Bore a Hand" (*Harper's Monthly*, April 1900) is a lightly humorous story about the loyalty of a soldier, a trumpeter and orderly named Oestreicher, who has spent most of his army time serving his major and the major's family. He fought with the major in the Apache wars and saved his life in Cuba. When the major, now a colonel, declares his faithful servant too old and orders him to stay at home before the campaign to the Philippines, the orderly smuggles himself aboard the troopship. The troops grin, knowing he would turn up sooner or later. The orderly saves his master one more time, and he is at last killed in the battle of Cabanatuan, dying in the arms of his weeping colonel.

"A Gallant American Officer" (*Collier's*, 7 April 1900) is a grittily realistic account of a courageous cavalry officer. Colonel Luther R. Hare, a graduate of West Point, now serving in the Philippines, had been virtually everywhere the action was: the battles of Little Big Horn and Wounded Knee, the pursuit of Billy the Kid, and the Chicago riots. He organized a volunteer regiment, the First Texas Cavalry, for the Cuban campaign, one of several that never got to Cuba. In the Philippines he has recently led a pursuit that lasted for weeks, in increasingly desperate conditions, at last resulting in the rescue of troops who had been taken prisoner. Only Colonel Hare's indomitable willpower could have kept his men courageous to the end.

"How the Worm Turned" (*Collier's*, 4 May 1901) returns to the Buffalo Soldiers, the subject of Remington's first military article more than 10 years earlier. The incident is told by an old Negro trooper of a group of cavalrymen, stationed at Fort Concho, Texas, who rode into town and shot it out with a bunch of Texans who had murdered one of their comrades. It is a somewhat embellished account of an actual West Texas incident, with Remington reaffirming the courage and loyalty of the Negro trooper.

From Remington's childhood passion for horses and from his pride in his father's record as a bold cavalryman in the Civil War came his intense interest in the soldier on horseback. As he engaged in his long series of assignments for *Harper's* and other magazines to illustrate and write about the West, it was the lives and experiences of individual soldiers that first caught his imagination. He saw them as a vanishing breed, and he wanted to keep alive both the image of dashing cavalry and heroic deeds and equally that of hardworking troopers loyal to their service.

Chapter Three

Indians

For most Americans, the name Frederic Remington evokes pictures and sculptures of horses, cowboys, and Indians, those emblems of a West that was rapidly vanishing by the close of the nineteenth century. Throughout his writings, both in his journalism and later in his fiction, Remington was keenly interested in Indian culture and in the problems of governmental policy.

Initially, however, Remington saw his pictures of Indians as a practical means of gaining entry into magazine illustration. His trip to the wilds of Arizona in 1885 had produced sketches of Indians that were accepted by *Harper's Weekly*. The first to appear over his own signature was a frontispiece plate, *The Apache War: Indian Scouts on Geronimo's Trail* (*Harper's Weekly*, 9 January 1886). The second, on 20 January, was *The Apaches Are Coming*. In June 1886, he went again to Arizona, this time sent by Henry Harper to illustrate the army's pursuit of Geronimo, an assignment he diverted to the illustration of soldiering. Later that year he began the illustrations for the last five installments of Lieutenant John Bigelow's *After Geronimo* for *Outing* magazine (December 1886 to April 1887).

In May 1887 an assignment took him to the Canadian West to sketch the Blackfoot Indians, his illustrations appearing in *Harper's Weekly* for more than a year. The trip also produced two works of art that received recognition: A watercolor, *Arrest of a Blackfoot Murderer,* appeared in the American Water-Color Society exhibit of January 1888, and an oil, *Return of a Blackfoot War Party,* was exhibited in the 63rd Annual Exhibition of the National Academy of Design in May 1888.

Remington's first extensive observation of Indians came about in 1888 when *Century* magazine's editor, Richard Watson Gilder, assigned him to write about as well as to illustrate the "wild tribes" of Indian Territory, in contrast to the "civilized" tribes east of the Mississippi. In his article "On the Indian Reservations" (*Century,* July 1889), Remington shares the common view of Indians as savages, but by the end of the journey, he had begun to see the problems of the tribes who have lost their lands and been herded into reservations.

The article begins with his recollection of the Apache Indians he had observed near the San Carlos Agency in Arizona some years earlier, when Geronimo was on the loose. One night, when Remington was encamped with two prospectors, they were startled when three Apaches appeared on the opposite side of the fire. The Indians wanted only flour, which the men gave them in generous quantities, but the experience was a warning. "Apaches are wont to lurk about in the rocks and chaparral with the stealth of coyotes, and they have always been the most dangerous of all the Indians of the Western country. They are not at all valorous in their methods of war, but are none the less effective" (*CW,* 31). Only a rigorous military system has kept them in the confines of the San Carlos reservation.

From these reminiscences, the article moves to the San Carlos Agency in the Gila River country in Arizona. The agency is administered by a Captain Bullis of the 24th Infantry, a Negro regiment. The captain has had years of experience leading Apache scouts and pursuing Apache braves and thus does not "fear the beetle-browed pack of murderers with whom he has to deal" (*CW,* 32). The agency is an oasis in a geographic and cultural desert. In spite of the scorching desert heat, Remington has a pleasant time enjoying the company and the excellent food prepared by the Chinese cooks.

The next day is ration day, and the Apaches have come from many miles in every direction. Although they did not like to be sketched, he manages to get some quick scenes before arousing their suspicion. There were hundreds of ponies, fantastically caparisoned; young girls with ornaments in their hair, in token of their virginity; tall Yuma bucks galloping about and gathering great chunks of beef that a native butcher threw to them, while Indian scouts preserved order. He notes that these Indians have natural dignity but little sense of social responsibility. On ration day, it was the duty of Captain Bullis to hold court to settle disputes. While the parties involved eyed one another with villainous hate, the captain calmly "relegated certain offenders to the guardhouse, granted absolute divorces, and probated wills with a bewildering rapidity" (*CW,* 33). More serious crimes—killing, carrying off women, or feuding—seldom came before the agent if the parties thought they could better adjust their own difficulties by the blood atonement process. Remington is told that the people steal the rations of the infirm and aged and leave them to starve on the agency doorstep. The Apache horses are ill fed and banged about by their savage masters. The fine blankets and articles of Mexican manufacture on their saddles were

CHEYENNE BUCK, DRAWING BY FREDERIC REMINGTON (1901)
Courtesy National Cowboy Hall of Fame, Oklahoma City (catalog no. 77.26.1).

probably stolen. The Indians forage into Mexico for many items, since they have little native manufacture except that of the women, who make excellent wickerwork and water jars, which they sell cheaply. The women also cut hay with knives and haul it on their backs for miles to sell to the army.

The article ends with a shift to an idyllic evening on the Gila River, where some members of the San Carlos tribe practice simple agriculture in an area where access to water makes this possible. They live in cool, leafy bowers above the river and farm the bottom lands. At evening the men and women open the irrigation gates and turn the water over the parched ground to nourish the corn, wheat, and vegetables. Signal rifle shots echo down the valley, like a curfew tolling the knell of parting day. Work horses are turned loose to graze. A procession of men and women carry water jars to their simple dwellings on the bluff. Remington can almost imagine Millet's peasants, but he knows these Indians are far from civilized. It grows dark, and he hears the measured thump of a tom-tom and a wild voice in strange sounds coming from a circle of half-naked forms around a fire, engaged in a religious ritual for the success of the growing crops.

Having within 24 hours seen the Apache transmuted from the beetle-browed savage to a feast-day reveler, from man before the social contract to Cherbourg peasants, and back to aborigine, Remington concludes with a statement for which he was sometimes later criticized. Citing what seemed to the white man the obvious incongruities in the lives of the Indians, he states that "no man can ever penetrate the mystery of their minds or explain the reason of their acts" (*CW,* 35). His intent here is not pejorative. He is merely observing.

The second part of the article presents an explicit contrast between the Apaches and the Comanches. Remington travels in a wagon to Fort Sill, Oklahoma, through stretches of green grass, a relief from the burning sands of Arizona. He marvels at the Red River and the groves of trees that grow along it. Fort Sill is built of stone, in a square around a parade ground of grass. Pole sheds and the timber of a nearby creek look invitingly cool.

At the fort, Remington meets the interpreter, who gives him welcome information about the tribe. Each Comanche, he is told, is named after some object in nature, and when one dies, the name of the object is changed and the old word is never spoken again. The Comanches, it seems, are great travelers, some to California, some as far south as Central America. They also speak Spanish and often have Mexican blood, "the result of stolen Mexican women, who have been ingrafted into the tribe" (*CW,* 36). Remington, with his love of horses, is gratified to learn that the Comanches take excellent care of their horses, handling them with good sense and intelligence, and in trading them, are the equal of Yankee horse traders.

Although the Comanches still live in their traditional movable lodges, they scorn the Shawnees, who may live in houses but do not keep their dwellings in "civilized" condition. The Comanches enjoy white-man conveniences such as umbrellas, baby carriages, and hats, and they often leave their rifles at home when they go out, although they like a Colt around the waist. There are the usual corps of scouts, Comanche and Kiowa, and they perform more functions than the Apache scouts, including the pursuit and arrest of Texas cowboys who come into the Territory to steal cattle and sell "corn juice."

The highlight of Remington's visit is the horse race to celebrate the Fourth of July, one of "the white man's big Sundays," for which the Indians have a high regard. Betting precedes the race. Inside a ring of mounted guards, Indians and cowboys wager silver dollars, guns, and other items. An elder of the tribe holds the stakes. Texans whisper among themselves, but the Indians are as "unmoved in countenance as oysters" (*CW*, 38), as gamblers ought to be. The favorite in the race is a bay stallion that has never been beaten, but the race is won by a young boy, half Comanche, half Mexican, riding a roan pony. As he rides back to his father, his face is calm, befitting his dignity as a young runner.

Remington admires the spirit of Indians like these and deplores the inevitable encroachment on their way of life:

> Far be it from these quaint people ever to lose their blankets, their horses, their heroism, in order to stalk behind a plow in a pair of canvas overalls. . . . I have confidence they will not retrograde. They can live and be successful as a pastoral people but not as sheepherders, as some great Indian department reformer once thought. . . . The Commanches travel about and move too fast for sheep; but horses and cattle they do have and can have, as long as they retain possession of their lands. But if the Government sees fit to consecrate their lands to the 'man with the hoe,' then, alas! good-bye to all their greatness. (*CW*, 38)

By the following year, what he feared had taken place. At noon on 22 April 1889, over 15,000 homesteaders lined up and raced for land in what would become Oklahoma Territory. It was an event that became a part of the family history of biographer Marquis James and a spectacular scene in the 1931 film of Edna Ferber's novel *Cimarron* (1930). The Comanches and other tribes lost the portions of their land that had not previously been allocated to the Indians, a continuing process that Remington sees as regrettably inevitable.

The injunction against sheep raising in the passage above is not merely Remington's attempt to dissociate himself from his own inglorious pastoral venture. The "man with the hoe" is a reference to Millet's 1863 painting, not to Edwin Markham's 1898 poem. Remington is referring to a figure in the state of human progress, not to an atavistic figure in the brutalization of labor. Remington is reflecting here the widely held view of the three stages of civilization. Regarded as "scientific," the theory held that all human societies pass through successive stages, each with its distinctive mode of subsistence and related institutions: savagery was the hunting stage, barbarism the pastoral, and civilization the agricultural. Each stage, symbolized respectively by the hunter with a spear, the herdsman with a staff, and the farmer with a hoe, provided gauges to determine the cultural progress of a society.

Thus, Remington uses the word "savage" for the Apaches, but the Comanches are clearly "barbarian." They are pastoral and nomadic. They live in tents. They are travelers, breed horses, and are sharp traders. They buy white man's products, sport Colt revolvers like the Texans, and love to gamble. They are in an advanced stage of barbarism, living in relative splendor.

The article closes with a brief and dismissive account of three other "wild" tribes that Remington visited briefly on the way to Fort Reno. Always keenly interested in the Indians' houses and modes of dwellings, he uses this as a sort of measuring stick of their advancement. The Kiowa, he notes, farm more than the other tribes visited but are not attractive people. They have been given houses but use them as outbuildings and live in tepees. The Wichitas live in grass houses, surrounded incongruously with wagons, agricultural implements, and cattle, but with no farming visible. The Territory Apaches are good-looking but regarded with contempt by other Indians and by traders. They live in tepees and gamble with cards, their faces gleaming with greed and cunning. Remington remarks that anyone who would "undertake to make Christian gentlemen and honest tillers of the soil out of this material would contract for a job to subvert the process of nature" (*CW,* 38).

It seems evident, he implies, that Indians do not follow the accepted theory of inevitable progress. To become civilized requires farming; yet many tribes engage in farming without reaching that final stage of development. Two popular theories of the day might account for this. Elsewhere in his writings, Remington refers to phrenology, citing the Indians' highly developed instinct of locality and their "psychic impulse" that could lead them unerringly to animals or men in hiding. There is no evidence that he ever felt the cranial bumps of any Indian, but it is reasonable to assume that a well-developed sense of direction and location would have been more useful to a hunter than to a farmer. The second "scientific" explanation could lie in the popular notion of "atavism," a regression that might be induced by the psychic damage of catastrophe, defeat, failure, and the like. Thus, people might "retrograde," descending from civilization to barbarism to savagery. This was the theory behind Remington's statement, quoted earlier, that the Comanches would not retrograde if they could keep their lands.

By the end of the century, the bestial stage of atavism was often lycanthropic, as in Kipling's "The Mark of the Beast," Frank Norris's *Vandover and the Brute,* and John Neihardt's "The Alien," not to be confused with the split personality of Stevenson's Jekyll and Hyde. By the 1920s it became part of popular psychology, in such works as Eugene O'Neill's *The Emperor Jones* or Vachel Lindsay's "Congo."

"Artist Wanderings among the Cheyennes" (*Century,* August 1889) continues Remington's account of his tour of Indian Territory with a four-day stop at the Cheyenne/Arapaho reservation near Fort Reno. On the way, he stops at a group of lodges of the Arapaho, where Remington admires a member of the tribe who had the finest profile he had ever seen. "He was arrayed in the full wild Indian costume of these latter days, with leggings, beaded moccasins, and a sheet wrapped about his waist and thighs" (*CW,* 39).

At Fort Reno, they find lodging at the trading post, where the colonel, once he has determined that Remington is neither "a Texas horse thief nor an Oklahoma boomer" (*CW,* 40), introduces him to an interpreter named Clark, and they set off to tour among the Cheyennes, a tribe that Remington comes to admire above all others.

His guide tells Remington something of the background of the Cheyennes. Of Algonquin origin, the tribes came from the far north, with a legend of "medicine arrows" given to them by an old man in a cave, explaining their past victories and their present hard experiences. Now, only a very few old men can tell perfectly the tribal stories. At the reservation, Remington observes that the Cheyennes are tall men with fine Indian features. They have adopted the Western cow-saddles, and they ride splendidly. At the Cheyenne camp near the fort, he finds a typically busy village. The green, level prairie is dotted with brown and white canvas lodges. Pony herds are scattered on the plain. A group of men squat in front of a lodge; a young girl runs away laughing when Remington draws her picture; the squaws are unusually good-looking, with pleasant-sounding names; a medicine man is at work over a sick person; young men are preparing for a dance; children are playing with dogs; women are beading moccasins; men are playing monte.

At the home of the old chief Whirlwind, they talk for hours through the interpreter. Remington wants to hear about the old Indian life before the wars, but Whirlwind wants to talk about their present problems. He has just returned from a conference with the Cherokees, where he was respectfully received. All the tribes fear the loss of their lands, and the council advises that they do nothing to weaken their tenure. The chief is too old to give up the old ways, but his son will be civilized like the Cherokee. The boy has had three years of schooling, wears white man's clothing, and has been a scout at the fort. He has been taught to sow and reap, but the old chief merely shrugs. The land is too dry for farming.

This triggers for Remington a dissertation on the current controversy over the government's Indian policy. Trying to turn the tribes into farmers, Remington argues, is useless when the area where they live is not productive. Both white men and Indians have tried to farm the land and failed where there is not enough rainfall. They cannot build cattle herds because the beef ration is insufficient, and they have to kill their breeding stock in order to survive. Sending a few children away to school, although not reprehensible, is of no use. They return with English, school clothes, short hair, and a trade they have no chance of employing. Every disinterested person, Remington declares, knows that the Indian Department should have been attached to the War Department. Indians are by nature good soldiers. They make splendid irregular cavalry. If organized as the Russian Cossacks are, they would do the United States much good and would become gradually civilized. An irregular cavalry becomes more important every year, and the corps of Indian scouts now do most of the police work in the West.

Unlike what he had to say about the Comanches, this disquisition on the Cheyennes is not encumbered with philosophic commentary. The Indian's failure in agriculture is a matter of climate, not a "regression" or the result of any "instinct" peculiar to the red man. Nevertheless, the basic points of the two reports are the same: Indian policy is wrongheaded. Indians should be under the jurisdiction of the army; they should not be forced into agriculture, while soldiering would be a useful and rewarding occupation for them.

Historically, the Cheyennes had been traders, but competition from white traders had destroyed much of their prosperity. The buffalo had been essential to both their subsistence and their economy. Their confinement on a reservation simply finalized the destruction of their economy and culture.

This destruction was evident in the beef-rationing incident that Remington now describes at Fort Reno. At San Carlos, he had seen the Apaches come to the agency as to a party; a butcher cut the beef into chunks, and the women carried it home. At Reno, among the Cheyennes, the rationing has become a brutal game, with the agency and the army as referees. The Indians assemble on the nearby plain. Cowboys working for the beef contractor drive the cattle into a large corral and brand them to identify them as government issue. An Indian policeman assigns a steer to each Indian recorded in his book, and the Indian marks his steer with some mutilation. The young men line up. At a signal, the cattle are driven out onto the plain, and the men chase the maddened steers and shoot them, sometimes erratically, requiring several shots to make the kill.

Remington is at first reminded of the traditional buffalo hunt, observing that the sport is evidently greatly enjoyed by the young men. In the end, however, he sees no pride in the activity. Certainly, to the Indians, chasing government-allocated beef does not compare with the old days of the buffalo hunt. In his novel *Dance Back the Buffalo* (1959), Milton Lott uses just such a cattle chase to symbolize the fallen state of a once-proud people.[1]

Late in the following year, in "Indians as Irregular Cavalry" (*Harper's Weekly,* 27 December 1890), Remington develops in detail his proposed solution to the Indian problem, suggested in the earlier discussion of the Cheyennes. On a journey with the Northern Cheyenne scout corps, escorting General Miles and a Peace Commission in Montana, Remington was impressed with what he had seen of the scout corps and reiterates his attack on the illogical policy of forcing the Indians into farming in the arid plains country. Under these conditions, the wild tribes are steadily retrograding: "With the healthy occupations of the hunter gone, they draw their rations listlessly, which having eaten, they starve, and in idleness their minds, morals, and bodies degenerate from lack of use" (*CW,* 60).

He points out that Indians are natural horsemen and have been used successfully as irregular troops from the French and Indian wars to the Indian wars in the West. The solution is to organize them, like the Cossacks, into several irregular cavalry regiments, each with companies of 100 men. Each company would have its own permanent village, located near appropriate agricultural or stock-raising operations. Officers from the regular army would serve as village chiefs and military commanders. Each soldier would be given clothing and regular rations for himself and his family until the village became self-sufficient. Each company would be light cavalry, with two horses per man and with pack trains.

It was a grandiose but impractical proposal. Assuming, as Remington did, that five such regiments were formed, it would constitute a force equal to one-half of the existing regular cavalry. The plan, he declares, would benefit white and Indian alike. Although he could suggest no other "industry" for the villages than agriculture and stock raising, he was confident they would succeed because "an Indian will do the most arduous and laborious work if he has a cavalry uniform on" (*CW,* 64).

His argument was soon invalidated, however, for the article appeared only a matter of days before the battle of Wounded Knee, which marked both the end of the Indian wars and the end of the army's control over the Indians. In any case, Remington's proposal was pure romanticism. He had felt genuine concern for the Indians' plight and their loss of pride, but what exercised his imagination were visions of hard-riding Indians in ethnic uniforms (for which he provided illustrations) and the image of Cossacks, who like Bedouin Arabs had their own local color and systems of military tactics. In his scheme for regeneration, he wanted to preserve the spirit of the old warrior days of the Indian.

This urge to protect and regenerate the Indian is reflected in what Remington wrote about their religion and mythology. He not only doubted the value of sending Indian children away to schools to learn "English, morals, and trades," he suggested that Christian teaching largely left them with no "mission in life beyond waiting for death" (*CW,* 60). Such sentiments were at odds with what had become the official policy not only of mission schools but of reservation boarding schools.

To Remington, myth, legend, ceremony, dress, and dialect gave color and life to a people. In the Cheyenne legend of the Medicine Arrows, the loss of the mythic arrows that gave the tribe valor and strength explains the latter-day travails of the people. Younger members of the tribe do not fully understand the ceremony because the Indians have seen and heard so much through the white men that their faith in their own traditions is shaken.

"The Great Medicine-Horse: An Indian Myth of the Thunder" (*Harper's Monthly,* September 1897) recounts a legend of the Absarokee of western Montana. The first of five stories featuring Sun-Down Leflare, a half-breed Indian, the story shows considerable narrative talent as well as a nice touch for humor. The character Sun-Down was modeled on the French Canadian guide L'Hereux, who had served as interpreter on Remington's trip into the Blackfoot country in early 1890 (Samuels, 258).

The narrative method is amusing. The story purports to be told by an old Indian who thinks a lot and speaks a little, with Sun-Down translating in a mixture of métis patois, pidgin, and contemporary slang, and inserting his own interpretations, while Remington as narrator tries to move the story along. The legend is that the Absarokees made a long trip south and stole many horses, among them a red horse, which they installed in their lodge. While there, the red horse exerts great power: the horses have many red colts, the women have many babies, the buffalo come close to the lodges, the Absarokees defeat every tribe that tries to steal the horse. One day the red horse quarrels with the medicine man, kills him, and becomes chief medicine man. On one occasion, he leaves the village and is persuaded by a virgin to return. Then one day he rises up to the sky to fight the great Thunder-Bird; sometimes now old men see him in pursuit, with lightning flashing from his nostrils. He will return someday and bring many buffalo, roll the land over the white man, and fight the north wind, when the Absarokees stop wearing pants and riding with saddles, and when they keep their women "on de square" (*CW,* 267).

Remington reveals the blending of folkloric and mythic material through Sun-Down's insistence upon explaining what the old Indian "really means" and explicating such terms as "medicine," "medicine lodge," and "medicine man," sometimes by comparison with Christian concept or ritual. Sun-Down was raised as a Catholic but holds to a belief in native medicine lore. Thus he can compare Indian incantation to a Latin mass and draw a lesson in Christian sexual morality from a fertility legend.

Like the Cheyenne legend, the legend of the Great Medicine-Horse tells of lost or diminished medicine and lost happiness, and of a hope that through ceremony or return to the "right way," the people will be regenerated.

That the earth would roll over the white man and the buffalo would return were central tenets of the "Ghost Dance," a messianic belief that caused considerable consternation in the period before the battle of Wounded Knee in 1890. Among the Sioux, the religion taught by the Paiute mystic named Wovoka took militant form. Indians who wore the Ghost Shirts and learned to perform the dance would be immune to the white man's bullets and would be magically raised into the air while the white men and all his works were buried beneath the ground.[2] Thousands of Indians flocked to the new religion, to the alarm of the government. It was the massacre at Wounded Knee that put an end to the fantasy, when bullets proved all too tragically effective, but the hope of a return to their own way of life was not extinguished.

"Sun-Down's Higher Self" (*Harper's Monthly,* November 1898) recounts how Sun-Down's native "medicine" (his secret magic) was superior to the advice of the white man's priest. His medicine saved him from a prairie fire by telling him which way to run: "Ah-h, firs time I evair gut my medicine she save my life—what? . . . Eef dose pries be' dair, she tell, 'you get ready for die'; but I no wan die" (*CW,* 333). Christianity could offer only acceptance of death, whereas Indian medicine offered an alternative.

"The Spirit of Mahongui" (*Harper's Monthly,* June 1998) purports to be a document written by a Frenchman in the French and Indian wars. Among his adventures, he hears the Indians' argument about the afterlife. Invoking the spirit of their great warrior Mahongui, one of the elders asks why they should believe the white man. All good things come from mother earth (fish, corn, fruits), the elder says, and all bad things come from the sky (burning sun, winds, rain, lightning, sickness), yet the Christian God lives in the sky and white men want us to go there when we die. Sternly, he declares, "For my part, I will not go there" (*CW,* 314). It did not profit the Indian if he salvaged his soul and lost his spirit.

By the close of the century, Remington had developed a keen sympathy for Indians' holding to the old ways and nurturing their diminished medicine. His finest tribute to this principle appeared in his novel *The Way of an Indian.* Peggy and Harold Samuels provide evidence that the novel was completed in the summer of 1900, although it was not published until five years later. Intended for publication by William Randolph Hearst in a magazine he planned to acquire, it was 1905 before Hearst purchased *Cosmopolitan,* and *The Way of an Indian* finally appeared. It was serialized in five installments, from November 1905 to March 1906, reprinted in hardcover in 1906, and was accompanied by brilliant illustrations, many in full color.

The novel movingly traces the progress of a warrior from boyhood to old chief. At the height of his position he is a symbol of the Cheyennes in all their military glory; his death is the fall of the Cheyenne warriors and the decline of a culture.

The Way gave Remington the opportunity to portray the "real" Indian, to offset the Indian of "misguided reformers" such as Hamlin Garland, who had taken up the cause of the Indian in *The Captain of the Gray-Horse Troop* (1902) and other stories. Garland supported the policy of "leading the Indians to happiness in an agricultural utopia" (Samuels,

328). For Remington, it was necessary to portray the Indian whose ways fit the world he lived in, the Indian who gave as good as he got, the Indian who could grow to respected old age, the Indian before he lost his medicine. Remington chose the Northern Cheyennes for his tribe, beginning the novel at a time when they were rich, powerful, and proud. Although he gives no dates nor names any incident, it is possible to set the novel by events within the stories. It begins some time between 1834 and 1849 when Fort Laramie was a trading post and ends with recognizable battles of 1876. Within that period the gradual decline of the Indian culture is traced. At the beginning the only contest with whites ("Yellow Eyes") is with traders; then the wagon trains and the railroads cross the treaty lands and the white hunters slay the Indians' buffalo by millions for their hides. Finally, the army with infantry, artillery, and cavalry march against the Sioux and Cheyennes, to their ultimate defeat.

The Way of an Indian is a short novel of eight chapters, each relating a stage in the life of the hero, whose name changes with each advancement toward becoming the chief of his tribe. Known as White Otter in boyhood, he goes on a quest to the "sacred place," fearing the power of the Bad God: "He was in mortal terror—every tree spoke out loud to him; the dark places gave back groans, the night-winds swooped upon him, whispering their terrible fears. The great underground wildcat meowed from the slopes, the red-winged moon-birds shrilled across the sky, and the stone giants from the cliffs rocked and sounded back to White Otter, until he cried aloud: 'O Good God, come help me' " (*CW,* 556). A little brown bat, sent by the Good God, saves him and becomes his "medicine."

When the boy, filled with the blood thirst made holy by the Good God, makes his first kill and brings back a scalp, he is known as the Bat. His next advancement comes when he bargains with a white trader to acquire a gun in return for ponies. The traders try to cheat him, and Bat defies them in the presence of the tribal council:

> The boy warrior stood with arms dropped at his sides, very straight in the middle of the tent, the light from the smokehole illumining the top of his body while his eye searched the traders. . . . "I will tell the white man how he can have his ponies back. He can hand over to me now the bright new gun which lies by his side. . . . I will not say again. I have spoken." (*CW,* 568)

The passage is accompanied by a striking illustration.

"I WILL TELL THE WHITE MAN HOW HE CAN GET HIS PONIES BACK,"
PAINTING BY FREDERIC REMINGTON (1905)
Photoengraving Courtesy Peggy and Harold Samuels.

The Bat's final step to manhood comes when he acquires a squaw. He rescues the girl from the half-breed trader who had abused her. In a daring elopement, she slides down a rope and they gallop away to freedom.

In a series of warrior raids with his tribe, the Bat's prowess earns him the name "Fire-Eater," and eventually he becomes the tribal chief.

In the last two chapters of the novel, Remington wrote what he did best, stories based upon historical incidents. In chapter 7 the Fire-Eater rides with Cheyennes and Sioux as they wipe out a white general and his cavalry on the summit of a hill, clearly General Custer and his Seventh Cavalry on the Little Big Horn River, 25 June 1876. Here Remington is telling the great mythic battle of the Indian wars from the viewpoint of a native warrior, to whom it was a wild, chaotic ride, full of excitement and the triumph of victory.

Although it lasted less than an hour, Custer's last stand has been the subject of more paintings, movies, and controversy than any single battle in Western American history. Remington made three versions of the event: a schoolboy imitative drawing in 1877; the painting *Last Stand,* in 1890, giving the traditional view of a cluster of white soldiers on the

rocky apex of a hill; and his 1903 painting *Custer's Last Fight,* showing
the battle from the Indian point of view, with mounted Indians in the
foreground, stripped for battle, firing at little stick figures on a far distant hill, with one figure in white barely distinguishable.[3]

The final chapter of *The Way of an Indian* is based on a brutal incident
in the later 1876 campaign to kill or capture the hostile Cheyennes and
Sioux to avenge Custer and the Seventh Cavalry. Some 400 Cheyenne
warriors and their families took refuge in a canyon of the Red Fork of
the Powder River. On 25 November, 1,100 troopers and scouts under
Colonel Ranald S. Mackenzie charged into the village. After a half day
of savage fighting, the Cheyennes escaped on foot with what food and
clothing they could salvage and fled north toward the camp of Crazy
Horse in northern Montana. In the devastating cold, several babies froze
to death on the first night out (Utley, 275–76).

Remington's story parallels the historical account. The Cheyennes
withdraw into "a deep gorge of the Big Horn Mountains" (*CW,* 591).
When the soldiers attack, some fight at the end of the village, others
take a position on the rim of the canyon. When the soldiers charge, Fire-
Eater escapes, carrying his son and his rifle, but cannot retrieve his
magic brown bat. Without his medicine, he is no longer protected from
harm. He reaches the snow-covered rim and joins the retreat to a
canyon where fires have been kindled, but his son is dead in his arms:
"The Fire Eater sat alone, waiting for the evil spirits . . . to come and
take him. He wanted to go to the spirit land where the Cheyennes of his
home and youth were at peace in warm valleys, talking and eating"
(*CW,* 596).

Fire-Eater's wish was the old Absarokee prophecy of the Great Medicine Horse: He will come back from the spirit world, roll the land over
the white man, bring plenty of buffalo, and fight the north wind.

In an interview in 1907, two years after the novel came out, Remington remarked that he had written "with the deliberate view of educating
men and women, who knew not the West, to a certain standard of
appreciation for its beauties, its fascinations, its intrinsic worth."[4] Ben
Merchant Vorpahl notes, however, that Remington's intent may have
been to show what the West was like, but if so, the illustrations he made
for the book did not follow this plan. "Instead, the sixteen pictures
Remington made to illustrate his story represented only sixteen different
views of the story's hero as he passed from youth to age. For all they said
about the region of the West, they might have had plain, undecorated
pasteboard for a backdrop" (Vorpahl 1978, 276). In short, Remington's

focus in the novel was not on the milieu of the West but directly on the life experience of his young Indian hero. John Seelye sees *The Way,* with its "emphasis on the harsh, even cruel, aspects of Indian character," as an antidote to Longfellow's *Hiawatha,* with its "essentially domestic, sentimental, and quasi-Christian emphases." By his realistic treatment of the Indian, Remington "put forth not only a sympathetic version of Indian life, but perhaps the most complex we have by a white man who was a contemporary witness to the red man's final decline and fall."[5]

The Cheyennes who fought with Fire-Eater at the Little Big Horn and in the canyon by the Big Horn mountains were the same Cheyennes who, under Dull Knife, fought hand to hand, man and woman, in the cold January of 1879 until Sergeant Carter Johnson, in "The Sergeant of the Orphan Troop," stopped the battle. Some of them were the old fighters Remington met when he traveled with the Miles Peace Commission, and the sons of some of them were the irregulars Lieutenant Casey commanded near Wounded Knee.

For his last work on the Indian, Remington had turned to the Cheyenne warrior, the symbol for him of the finest traits of the Indian culture. While recognizing the inevitability of the white man's march across the continent, he had moved from his initial view of the "savage" Indian to a deeply felt concern for the lost dignity of a once-proud people.

Chapter Four

Cowboys

Although the name Frederic Remington is widely associated with the cowboy, through his illustrations and especially through his sculpture, the cowboy is a less prominent subject in his published writings than the soldier or the Indian. As we have seen, Remington perpetuated the myth that he himself had been a cowboy, suppressing the fact that his only ranching experience was a 10-month venture in sheep raising in Kansas that ended in failure in 1885. Nevertheless, the cowboy was a key figure in the Western scene that formed the chief source of Remington's imaginative life, and along with Theodore Roosevelt and Owen Wister, he contributed to the popular lore of the cowpuncher.

In 1887, early in his career, Remington was pleased to be commissioned to illustrate Theodore Roosevelt's *Ranch Life and the Hunting-Trail* (1887), for which he could draw cowboys and horses. Both the text and the art portray the cowboy and his mount as the hard rider and the hard-ridden pony, not sentimentalized by either Roosevelt or Remington. The various types of cow pony—the bronco, the mustang, the cayuse, the pinto—were all notable for their endurance. As Remington wrote later in "Horses of the Plains" (*Century,* January 1889), the Indian pony is not "the bounding steed of romance. . . . He may be all that the wildest enthusiast may claim in point of hardihood and power, as indeed he is, but he is not beautiful" (*CW,* 18). However, to compensate, he has "an extra endowment of brains" (*CW,* 20). He may buck with great spirit when struggling with man for mastery, but once ridden, he is intelligent enough to conform.

Roosevelt's cowboys in *Ranch Life* work hard and play hard. Each man needs 8 to 10 horses during the working season; in the winter all but two of his horses are sent out to fend for themselves. There is no wanton cruelty, but horses are trained the hard way and driven recklessly up and down mountain sides in the roundup and on the hunting trips. Two of Remington's best-known bronzes evolved from his work in *Ranch Life. Painting the Town Red,* a drawing of four cowboys riding hard and firing revolvers in the air became, in 1902, a bronze of four similar cowboys titled *Coming through the Rye.* The drawing *The Bucking Bronco* and the 1895 bronze *The Bronco Buster* both represent the rough rider described by Roosevelt. Thus it was fitting that when Roosevelt's Rough Riders of the Spanish-American War disbanded, they presented him with a casting of *The Bronco Buster* (Samuels, 288).

Roosevelt depicted cowboys as for the most part honest, reliable, and hardworking. In his own writing, however, Remington initially portrayed cowboys of a different type. At Fort Sill, Oklahoma, in 1889, he found that one of the duties performed by the government-employed Kiowa and Comanche scouts was to "follow the predatory Texas cowboy who comes into the Territory to build up his fortunes by driving off horses and selling corn juice to the Indians" (*CW*, 36). He found also that many Indians needed to be reassured, on meeting a white stranger, that he was not a Texas cowboy.

In 1890, when Remington was with the army and Indians in Montana and the Badlands, he noted that cowboys had the reputation for violent action and for ignoring the law. A day or so after Christmas, while following the hostile Sioux with Lieutenant Casey's Cheyenne scouts, he and Wolf-Voice, an old Cheyenne scout, saw starving broncos abandoned by the hostiles. Wolf-Voice said, "Cowboy he catch'em." When Remington observed that the army had orders not to allow any citizens to cross the Cheyenne River, Wolf-Voice said, "Cowboy he no give um dam; he come alle samee" (*CW*, 73).

In fact, both Roosevelt's working cowboy and Remington's cattle-stealing, whisky-peddling cowboy existed. The carousing cowboy and the rustler were familiar subjects in the Eastern press, along with the more admirable types.

The immense popularity of Buffalo Bill's Wild West Show brought the horse and his rider into the realm of entertainment. After Remington's journey with Poultney Bigelow to Russia and Germany in the spring of 1892, he stopped briefly in England, where he saw the show. With his passion for horsemanship, he was entranced by the skill and daring of the wild, exotic riders. In "Buffalo Bill in London" (*Harper's Weekly*, 3 September 1892), he describes with enthusiasm the cosmopolitan cast of the show: Russian Cossacks, Argentine gauchos, Mexicans, Oglalas, Sioux, and American cowboys, an aggregate of wild humanity. Beyond mere entertainment, however, Remington sees the show as "a poetical and harmless protest against the Derby hat and the starched linen—those horrible badges of the slavery of our modern social system . . . where the greatest crime is to be individual, and the unpardonable sin is to be out of the fashion" (*CW*, 98).

In January 1893 *Harper's* commissioned Remington to write and illustrate articles on ranching in northern Mexico. He would be returning to the Southwest of the Apache war days and beyond into Mexico, a country that had fascinated him since he first went there in 1886. The day before he left, he wrote to Bigelow: "Tomorrow—tomorrow I start for 'my people'—d—— Europe—the Czar— . . . the conventionalities— . . . I go to the simple men—men with the bark on—the big mountains—the great deserts and the scrawny ponies—I'm happy."[1] The phrase "men with the bark on" came from the language of the trapper, where "bark" was hair, literally men who had kept their scalps (Samuels, 297). As a term for strong men surviving in a harsh land, the phrase was used by Harper's as the title of the third anthology of Remington's articles in its magazines.

For the assignment in Mexico, Remington spent about a month at the remote hacienda San Jose de Bavicora, some 225 miles northwest of Chihuahua, a five-day ride by coach. Now he sees cowboys in a favorable light, in contrast to the Texas marauders he described earlier. He is impressed by the owner and overseer of the ranch, whom Remington calls "Jack Gilbert." In the first of three ranching articles, "An Outpost of Civilization" (*Harper's Monthly*, December 1893), he gives an account of the history of the ranch as told to him by "Gilbert." It had been built in 1770 by the Jesuits. In 1840 the "good fathers" were murdered by the Apaches. The country was devastated and the ranch fell into ruin. Then in 1882, Gilbert, describing himself as an American cowboy, accompanied by two companions, went south from Arizona, looked over the fair plain of Bavicora, and said, "I will take this." By purchase he acquired the plains, moved in with his hardy punchers, fixed up Bavicora so it would be habitable, and chased the Indians off his ranch. Presently, when the Mexican vaqueros saw that the American could hold his own with the Apaches, they overcame their terror and came up to take service. There are now 200 men who work for him and "follow him on the Apache trail, knowing he will never run away, believing in his beneficence and trusting to his courage" (*CW,* 115).

This version of the facts is dramatic, but the actual story is somewhat more prosaic. Biographers Peggy and Harold Samuels point out that "Jack Gilbert" was in fact Jack Follansbee, who managed the ranch for California financier George Hearst (180). In 1884 Hearst had bought Bavicora, a working ranch of a million acres, including outlying ranches. When his son, William Randolph, declined to own or run the ranch, George turned it over to Jack Follansbee, William's college chum and social companion, to manage (Samuels, 180). Follansbee in turn left the management to subordinates for six months of each year and devoted himself to being a man-about-town in New York and a grandee when he was in Mexico. Whether the fictional account came from Follansbee himself or was embroidered by Remington, the man certainly was not a cowboy who rode down from Arizona. Remington, however, admired him and regarded him as one of "my people," a man "with the bark on."

Remington describes the Bavicora ranch as a colonial plantation, with its Anglo manager, overseers, bookkeeper, and native workers, but in its daily life it is also the traditional, self-contained Mexican rancho, with Jack Gilbert as the motive force of the enterprise. The work of the ranch is performed by the vaqueros, the Mexican cowboys, whom Remington came to admire, along with the Anglo-American *patron* and *administradors*. His admiration for this group resembles the enthusiasm he had felt for the Negro troopers of the 10th Cavalry and their officers some years earlier in Arizona. Like the troopers, the vaqueros are cheerful, respectful, and competent, and like Lieutenant Powhatan Clarke and his fellow officers, Jack Gilbert and his Anglo assistants extend cordial hospitality to their visitors. Both groups also share a common enemy—the Apache—from whom danger is an ever-present threat.

In this remote outpost of civilization, the vaquero must be a man of some hardihood. No doctor attends the sick or disabled. "At times instant and awful death overtakes the puncher—a horse in a gopher-hole, a mad steer, a chill with a knife, a blue hole where the .45 went in, a quicksand closing overhead," and in the end, "a cross on a hill-side" (*CW,* 118).

Yet the vaquero has his simple pleasures. The men make a game of practicing with the rope, at which they are extremely skillful. One evening during Remington's visit the *patron* gives a ball. The vaqueros all come with their girls and dance vigorously to the music of a string band, spurred on by visits to an adjoining room where a heavy jug of "strong-water" is provided. Sometimes the vaqueros offer to sing to the *patron.* Ironically, "the songs are all largely love and women and doves and flowers, in all of which nonsense punchers take only a perfunctory interest in real life" (*CW,* 119).

On the serious side, the Apache was a constant threat to both men and cattle. While Remington was there, men were detailed to roam the country in search of fresh trails of the cattle killers. If they found them, they did not hesitate to kill them. Mercy was not expected.

The second article in the series, "In the Sierra Madre with the Punchers" (*Harper's Monthly,* February 1894), gives an account of a trip to outlying ranches of the Bavicora. The trip provided the obligatory hunting and camping of Western ranch hospitality, a tour of the vast ranch, and an opportunity to observe the work of the punchers. It was a rigorous journey for a man of Remington's excessive weight, much like his scout with the Buffalo Soldiers a few years earlier. Long days in the saddle over steep mountain trails, nights of extreme cold, and limited rations all taxed his endurance, but he came through in triumph, as he had done before. There were pleasures on the trip as well. One rainy night before the campfire, a hunter told stories of past events, and the legend of the lost mine of Tiopa was narrated by a vaquero in the quiet manner of one whose memory goes far back and to whom it is all real.

The series closes with "A Rodeo at Los Ojos" (*Harper's Monthly,* March 1894), giving Remington the chance to describe a roundup at an outlying Bavicora ranch, held jointly with the ranch of San Miguel. As Remington portrays it, the roundup is both ranching function and sporting event, with form established by custom. With his love for excitement and physical action, nothing could please him more than a rodeo, and he narrates the day's work in some of his best pictorial prose.

Los Ojos is the hosting ranch, with its foreman as the *capitan* in charge. About mid-morning, a cavalcade of San Miguel men ride up and the Los Ojos men ride out to greet them with a "peculiar shoulder tap, or abbreviated embrace." With their terra-cotta buckskin clothing, heavy cowhide leggings, pistols, jingling spurs, and serapes tied behind their saddles, they are an impressive "cavalcade of desert scamperers" (*CW,* 132).

Extra horses are brought in and the punchers select their mounts by roping. A steer is butchered and the meat distributed to the men. As the sun is westering, the vaqueros are sent out into the hills and far out on the plain, where they build little fires, cook their beef, and spend the night, enveloped in their serapes. At early dawn they converge on the ranch, driving their stock before them.

In the morning, thousands of cattle are driven into the rodeo. Gradually they converge on the ground, and "hollow bellowings like the low pedals of a great organ" are heard. After a lengthy exchange of Spanish formalities, the *patron* of San Miguel and the captains of the neighboring ranches ride into a huge circle of cattle to estimate which cattle belong to them, to observe the brands, to inquire as to the condition of the animals and the number of calves and "mavericks" (unbranded calves), and to settle any disputes that may arise.

All controversy having been adjusted, some of the punchers hold the cattle in the circle while others ride into the apparently impenetrable mass, driving them into herds according to their brands. Remington describes with gusto the "matchless horsemanship of the punchers" (*CW*, 134). Men on little ponies manipulate huge bulls and frightened cattle, grabbing the tails of steers and throwing them head over heels, or roping and dragging them out of the circle of milling cattle. Out of this scene of blinding dust, bleating calves, bellowing cows, and lathered horses, the cowboy astonishingly creates order.

By high noon the branded cattle have been cut out into separate herds, and cows with mavericks are gathered in corrals. The men now turn to the corrals and the work of "cutting" (castrating) and branding. Here men go on foot into the corral, one man ropes a calf and drags it out of the mass of cows, two others "rastle" it to the ground, and another brands it. Occasionally an old cow takes an unusual interest in her offspring and charges boldly, to the amusement of the men. When the day's work is done, the men repair to the *casa* and indulge in games and pranks.

Remington points out that although the vaquero revels in the vigorous activity of the rodeo, he passively accepts his generally spartan existence. He works for 8 to 12 Mexican dollars a month and lives on a severely simple diet. He is *peoned* and in hopeless debt to his *patron*. He buys his gorgeous buckskin clothes, silver-mounted straw hat, riata, and *cincha* rings but makes his own rope lariat, buckskin boots, leggings, and saddle. The *patron* furnishes his arms. Half his year is spent at roundups; the rest he spends alone in outlying camp, to turn stock back onto the range. In the "camp," where a tree does duty as a house, he has his pack of "grub," his saddle and serape, a piece of sheet iron for a stove, and a piece of pottery for boiling.

In a lyric passage, Remington defines the vaquero:

> The *baile,* the song, the man with the guitar—and under all this *dolce far niente* are their little hates and bickerings, as thin as cigarette smoke and as enduring as time. They reverence their parents, they honor their *patron,* and love their *compadre.* They are grave, grave even when gay; they eat little, they think less, they meet death calmly, and it's a terrible scoundrel who goes to hell from Mexico. (*CW,* 136)

The two Anglo-American foremen on the Bavicora ranch are another type entirely, but portrayed by Remington in equally glowing terms.

They have all the "rude virtues," the "intelligence which is never lacking and the perfect courage which never fails." These two Texans, unlike those he has described earlier, are the superior of any "cow-men" he has ever seen. In a burst of romantic sentiment, he estimates their moral fiber and their character: "Modern civilization, in the process of educating men beyond their capacity, often succeeds in vulgarizing them; but these natural men possess minds which, though lacking all embellishment, are chaste and simple, and utterly devoid of a certain flippancy which passes for smartness in situations where life is not so real" (*CW,* 136–37). At the same time, these American punchers "are good friends and virulent haters, and, if justified in their own minds, would shoot a man instantly, and regret the necessity, but not the shooting, afterwards" (*CW,* 137). If this appears inconsistent with their "moral character," Remington's enthusiasm typically carries him to heights of exaggeration.

Remington of course did not discover the vaquero. Since the time of the Mexican War and the California gold rush, the Mexican cowboy had been familiar to readers. The English traveler Frank Marryat wrote of the vaqueros (whom he called "vaccaros") in his 1855 journal, on his visit to the Santa Rosa valley ranch of the Carrillo family.[2] The vaqueros' costume and equipment, their skill with the rope, and their reckless horsemanship, as described by Marryat, had changed little by 1893. What Remington added was a contribution to the mythic chronicle of the cowboy.

In 1892 Remington was employed in illustrating a new edition of Francis Parkman's *The Oregon Trail,* the historic account of Parkman's 1846 journey from St. Louis to California. In his introduction to the new edition, the venerable Parkman remarked, somewhat gloomily, that the trapper and the buffalo, having virtually disappeared into the past, were replaced by cattle and barbed wire fences and the cowboy (Vorpahl 1978, 275). Yet the cowboy, by this date half a century later, was in his turn nearing the end of his heyday.

When Remington and Owen Wister met by chance in Yellowstone Park in September 1893, it was the beginning of an association that would be mutually beneficial for a decade. Remington illustrated many of Wister's Western stories, and Wister often drew on Remington's knowledge of the West. One of the classics of cowboy lore, Wister's widely read essay "The Evolution of the Cow-Puncher" (*Harper's Monthly,* September 1895), was proposed by Remington. In 1894 he wrote to Wister, urging him to "make me an article on the evolution of the puncher—the passing as it were," indicating his assumption that the cowboy was already fading from the scene (Vorpahl 1972, 47). The letter continues with examples of ideas that could be worked into the article, sketching the cowboy from his beginning to his decline: "The early days 1865 to 1878 he was pure Texan &c——cattle boom he was rich—got $75 a month—wore fine clothes—adventurous young men from all parts went into it . . . . Cheyenne saddles—fine chaps—$15 hats—Fringed gloves—$25 boots &c. With the crash of the boom—Yankee ingenuity killed the cattle business as much as anything—the Chicago packers—the terrible storms, the drought &c." (Vorpahl 1972, 47).

Wister used many of Remington's notes in the final version of his essay, but beyond the details of the cowboy's life, Wister was keen on establishing his cultural and racial origin. For some time he had planned an essay, "The Course of Empire," a historical "study" with the cowboy as symbolic American in Western civilization. In Remington's proposal, he saw the vehicle for his study. In his *Ranch Life and the Hunting-Trail,* Theodore Roosevelt had suggested the Southeast as the origin of the cowboy: "The rough-rider of the plains, the hero of rope and revolver, is first cousin to the backwoodsman of the southern Alleghenies."[3] Remington saw the origin in the Mexican vaquero, from whom the Kentucky or Tennessee man had acquired the skills and attitudes of the cowboy.

Wister, however, wanted a more exalted source for his cowboy and moved his birthplace to England, where as an Anglo-Saxon, he was a man of the proper stuff. "Directly the English nobleman smelt Texas, the slumbering untamed Saxon woke in him . . . a born horseman, a perfect athlete, and . . . fundamentally kin with the drifting vagabonds who swore and galloped by his side" (Vorpahl 1972, 80).[4] No others would qualify as heroes of the glorious West, certainly not Poles nor Huns nor Russian Jews; Swedes settle to farming; the Frenchman is "at his best in a house"; "the Italian has forgotten Columbus, and sells fruit"; among the Spaniards and the Portuguese there was "no Cortez" (Vorpahl 1972, 80). Only the Anglo-Saxon was worthy.

Wister's cowboy is like a medieval armed knight. The roundup is a tournament, and just as the knights of Camelot prized their armor, so did the cowboy prize his pistol with its mother-of-pearl handle (Vorpahl 1972, 86).

In a flight of rhetoric, Wister traces his cowboy's westward migration: "Roving took him from his Norse crags across Albion," and then to America. He came to Texas, a new country full of grass and cattle and Mexicans by the hundred. He prospered, and word of his prosperity spread to other Saxons. The cowboy drove herds to Abilene and fought bands of Mexicans, Indians, and cattle thieves. He grew into a man unlike any other. This was the cowboy of the bonanza years, but he is no more.

On seeing the draft of Wister's essay, Remington remarked dryly, in a letter to Wister: "Strikes me there is a good deal of English in the thing—I never saw an English cowboy—have seen owners. You want to credit the Mexican with inventing the whole thing—he was the majority of the boys who first ran the steers to Abilene, Kansas" (Vorpahl 1972, 70). Wister obligingly inserted a short sentence, still unable to credit any race but the Anglo-Saxon: "Let it be remembered that the Mexican was the original cowboy, and the American improved on him" (Vorpahl 1972, 92).

For all their common interests, Remington and Wister spoke a different language. It was necessary to Wister's "course of empire" that his cowboy be Anglo-Saxon. Remington's view was practical and realistic. He was glad enough to illustrate the essay he had pressed Wister to write, but he never expressed warm enthusiasm for the result.

It is easy to believe that Remington's illustrations for the essay were more appealing to many readers than Wister's high-flown rhetoric. Some critics have expressed the view that "the pictures overpowered the text" (Samuels, 233). In a foreword to Vorpahl's *My Dear Wister,* Wallace Stegner compares Remington and Wister in their contributions to the "mythifying process" of the cowboy. Wister, he says, was "tuned in to literary and historical wavelengths," whereas Remington, although equally romantic, was "primarily an eye—a quick, accurate, unsentimental eye, and a hand that could record swiftly what the eye saw" (Vorpahl 1972, vii).

That the cowboy's day was ending, both Remington and Wister agreed. The free and open range was overstocked, with insufficient winter forage and shelter. The virgin pastures were exhausted, and wire fences increasingly enclosed the ranges. Storms and drought wrought havoc, and the Chicago meatpackers, led by P. A. Armour, controlled the industry. Populism and big money dominated the scene.

Wister suggests that the very nature of the cowboy's nomadic existence precluded his establishing heirs to his way of life. They "begot no sons to continue their hardihood" (Vorpahl 1972, 93). In the dance halls and saloons, they did not meet respectable women. They made war in plenty, but not love. The cowboy had no minstrel like Sir Walter Scott to sing of him, and he had "no Flora McIvor! Alas!" (Vorpahl 1972, 93).

Wister's reference to the beautiful and noble lady in Scott's *Waverly* gave Remington the theme for a down-to-earth illustration. The scene, depicting two cowboys parlaying with Indian women outside their lodges, is titled *There Was No Flora McIvor*. Clearly, sex was available, but not "love."

On a holiday visit to Florida in the same year, Remington encountered a type of cowboy that ran counter to every virtue he admired in the punchers of the West. "Cracker Cowboys of Florida" (*Harper's Monthly*, August 1895) gives a humorous account of a set of lazy, seedy, drunken cowpunchers whose principal occupation is stealing cattle by any method available. One young man describes how brands are changed, adding a larger circle around a smaller one, making an "I" into an "E," and so on. The townspeople keep their double-barreled shotguns at the ready when the cowpunchers are expected.

In "Life in the Cattle Country" (*Collier's*, 26 August 1899), Remington returns to praise of the cowboy's hardihood in the arid Western plains. Their numbers may have been decreasing, but those still active lived up to the highest standards of the past. He describes in realistic detail how the cattle are gathered from immense distances to the roundup, generating the same excitement he had felt at the Bavicora ranch in Mexico some years earlier. He is impressed, as always, by the facility of the men who throw the rope or lariat over the diving, plunging steer or bull. The men say that the greatest skill lies in throwing the noose so as to catch the fore or hind legs. "To throw the noose over the head or horns is a trick held in slight esteem" (*CW,* 388). Then the pony, who has been trained to the work, goes back on his haunches and awaits the shock of the taut rope when the capture is made.

In a characteristic defense of those he admires, Remington declares that the Western cowpunchers, "maligned and traduced as they have been, possess a quality of sturdy, sterling manhood which would be to the credit of any man in any walk of life. The honor of the average 'puncher' abides with him continually. He will not lie; he will not steal. He keeps faith with his friends; toward his enemies he bears himself like a man" (*CW,* 388).

Such was the image of the heroic cowboy created by Remington, Roosevelt, and Wister, an image that has dominated popular fiction and Hollywood films, an image that Wallace Stegner calls "the most imagination-catching and durable of our mythic figures" (Vorpahl 1972, vii).

Chapter Five
The Strenuous Life

Between 1887 and 1901 Remington published a number of sporting narratives, reflecting his enthusiasm for the turn-of-the-century cult of the "strenuous" life, akin to the turn of the present century's craze for "fitness."

Except for the early "Coursing Rabbits on the Plains," most of the items in this group were written for *Harper's Monthly*. For its more distinguished readership than that of the *Weekly*, Remington devoted special care to his writing, and these pieces are among his best literary achievements. They also offered opportunity for excellent illustrations and provided topics for fine paintings.

The sporting story was a popular literary form before Remington began his career. William F. Porter, editor of *Spirit of the Times*, a journal that ran from 1831 to 1861, published articles and narratives by American authors along the lines of the British sporting sketch but with American idiom, setting, and type of sport. Writers such as Thomas Bangs Thorpe (1815–1878), author of "The Big Bear of Arkansas" (1841), wrote these by the dozen, and even John James Audubon's *Ornithological Biography,* appearing in the 1830s, contained not only his drawings but also short accounts of his hunting experiences and sketches of rural sports.[1]

Traditionally the story had certain basic features: a defined geographical and social setting, with "local color"; a cast of participants and observers (often "outsiders"); an assemblage of horses and dogs, along with riding and hunting equipment; the rules or conventions of the sport; and some climactic incident. The relative merits of horses, dogs, guns, and saddles could be debated at length. Unusual rules, strange conventions, high stakes, and wild betting often heightened the action. Most sporting stories were serious, at least in intent, but the form lent itself to humor or parody, and with some exaggeration, the story could become the tall tale, as in Thorpe's "Big Bear" or Mark Twain's "Celebrated Jumping Frog of Calaveras County" (1865).

Since Remington's boyhood days in the woods and streams around Ogdensburg, he had loved the outdoor life of fishing, hunting, and canoeing. In his adult life, he regularly escaped from the confines of the city and the studio to join up with outdoor men of action, whom he called his "tribe," those "men with the bark on" who gloried in physical challenge. Many of his sporting narratives deal with the contrast between the "club" men, with their comfortable accommodations and their concern with the "rules" of the sport, and the "tribes" men, who cheerfully faced rough conditions and limited rations for the love of the activity itself.

Remington's first published piece, "Coursing Rabbits on the Plains" (*Outing,* May 1887), offers not one but two sporting stories, cleverly combined in a single incident from his days as a sheep rancher in Kansas. The first is a hilarious account of a rabbit hunt, spoofing the more respectable citizens of the community who, as members of the local chapter of the American Coursing Club, staged an annual meet where gentlemen on horseback and packs of greyhounds chased rabbits to the kill. Remington and his friends decide to play their own version of this simulated English fox hunt. Their coursers are a motley crew of ranchers and ranch hands, one wearing full English hunting regalia except for the red coat. They all carry six-foot poles, having added the requirement that the rider must strike the rabbit with his "lance." Each man uses his best horse, and with a "pack" of two dogs they chase rabbits through fences, in and out of "draws," and over hills. Of their two dogs, one is a greyhound, the other an old peg-legged but wiser dog, who quits the hunt in disgust. Men fall off their horses as they try to spear a bobbing and weaving jackrabbit. In the end, the net catch is one rabbit killed; a second escapes under a hayrick.

Remington now adds a second incident—a classic racetrack con story. The rabbit chase leads to the corral of "Old John" Mitchener, a new arrival from somewhere in the Indian Territory. The young ranchers, with their expensive horses, are taken in by the old codger, who claims he has not raced for 10 years and rings in a sleeper, a horse that looks like "an old brood mare" but which takes the lead and runs away with the race. The cocksure young ranchers, who believe *they* are provoking the race and setting the rules, lose out to the old man. As he takes over their horses, he tells them, "I've been a layin' fer you fellers ever since I came inter these yar parts and I reckon as how I've sort of got ye'" (*CW,* 9).

In "Coursing" Remington carefully avoids the mention of sheep, hoping as always that his ranching experience will be assumed to be with cattle, the more socially acceptable type of ranching.

The mock-heroic elements and the humorous self-deprecation in this first effort are characteristic of many of Remington's later works. The piece also establishes his lifelong fondness for physical adventure and challenge and reflects his joyous memories of the wild, careless days of "holiday" ranching. Even though Remington and his pals became the laughingstock of the town, being taken in by an old con man was good fun.

"Black Water and Shallows" (*Harper's Monthly,* August 1893), the source for one of Remington's finest paintings, gives a lively and sometimes lyric account of a canoe trip down the Oswegatchie River of upstate New York, reflecting Remington's affection for the natural beauties of the north woods and his rejection of the conventional "club" man's approach to hunting and fishing. His professional guide, known as "Has," is pleased but puzzled when Remington elects to cruise down a shallow and rocky river—which the lumbermen said could not be "run"—simply for the pleasure and challenge of the journey. Most of Has's customers no sooner enter the woods than they are "overcome with a desire to slay. No fatigue or exertion was too great when the grand purpose was to kill the deer and despoil the trout streams" (*CW,* 104).

The trip is not intended to be a comfortable outing. Physical endurance and challenge are ingredients in the life of the true sportsman. For Remington and his guide, the first day begins in the early morning. They row across a lake, portage around a dam and rapids at the head of the river, glide through a long stretch of still, dark water, occasionally impeded by a fallen tree, rush down steepening rapids, dodging boulders and floating logs, and tired, footsore, and hungry, go ashore and camp.

Recounting the tortures of the portage around the dam leads to a comparison of the philosopher and the sportsman. "The person who tilts back on a chair on the veranda of a summer hotel, while he smokes cigars and gazes vacantly into space, is your only true philosopher; but he is not a sportsman. The woods and the fields and the broad roll of the ocean do not beckon to him to come out among them. He detests all their sensations, and believes nothing holy except the dinner hour, and with his bad appetite that too is flat, stale, and unprofitable" (*CW,* 104–5).

The sportsman, however, is not mindless. "The long still water is the mental side of canoeing, as the rapid is the life and movement" (*CW,* 105). As they glide on the still water, Remington is enraptured. "The dark water wells along, and the branches droop to kiss it. In front the

BLACK WATER, PAINTING BY FREDERIC REMINGTON (1893)
Photoengraving Courtesy Peggy and Harold Samuels.

gray sky is answered back by the water reflection, and the trees lie out as
though hung in the air, forming a gateway, always receding. Here and
there an old monarch of the forest has succumbed to the last blow and
fallen across the stream" (*CW,* 105).

Then the river speeds up, the canoe glides more rapidly, the pipe is
laid to one side, the paddle is grasped firmly, and there is no talking.
Now it is paddle, and tumble from the boat to keep it afloat, and scram-
ble on loose stones to recover it when it breaks away, and bring it to
shore, a procedure that is constantly repeated. "Finally the coffee boils,
the tent is up, and the bough bed laid down. You lean against the dead
log and swap lies with the guide." All the great hunters, Remington
remarks, are magnificent liars. "A man who has not hunted considerably
can't lie properly without offending the intelligence of that part of his
audience who have" (*CW,* 107). In the Remington lexicon, the "sport"
tallies his kill, while the true sportsman (hunter or canoeist) and the
artist record and recall, and swap lies and spin yarns with a member of
the tribe.

In the 1890s there were still vast flocks of ducks and geese, herds of deer and elk, and enough bear to adorn the stately dens of the Atlantic and Pacific coasts. In the frontier days cowboys were not allowed to wear their guns in cattle towns, lest they shoot up windows and store signs. By the 1890s shooting rabbits, or any other game, on streets or rural byways, was prohibited. For the more genteel sportsmen, the formation of private gun clubs offered the advantages of private field or stream and encouraged the maintenance of hunting preserves on public land.

In 1888 Theodore Roosevelt brought the gun club and the preserve together with the formation of the Boone and Crockett Club, an organization of men devoted to "manly sport with the rifle" and "the preservation of the large game of this country."[2] Roosevelt went on to become America's mightiest hunter, slaying everything from mountain sheep to rogue bull elephants. His autobiography contains numerous accounts of determined stalking, unflinching encounter, and sufficient marksmanship, all portrayed as contributing to self-discipline and serving to build character, both individual and national.

Roosevelt made a significant contribution to the policy of preserving the national parks. Two Remington articles—"Policing the Yellowstone" (*Harper's Weekly*, 12 January 1895) and "Mountain Lions in Yellowstone Park" (*Collier's*, 17 March 1900)—support this view, dealing with the official efforts to keep hunting safe from poachers and predators in a popular hunting preserve. "Americans," he wrote, "have a national treasure in the Yellowstone Park, and they should guard it jealously" (*CW*, 175).

In "Stubble and Slough in Dakota" (*Harper's Monthly*, August 1894), Remington returns to the mildly satiric treatment of the "club" men. In "Black Water and Shallows" his guide was a "tribesman"; in "Stubble and Slough" he is in the company of "sports," those who seek comfort rather than adventure. The party consists of two old generals who interrupt conversations to recall old battles, a portly and officious phlebotomist from Philadelphia, a young officer from the regular army, and three young men from Harvard. Remington joined the group in August 1893 in Chicago, where he was touring the Columbian Exposition, and traveled with them by Pullman car to the wheatlands of North Dakota. From the Pullman they were taken daily by wagon to stubble fields and sloughs to shoot prairie chickens and ducks.

Such a trip was the 1890s American middle-class version of the traditional hunting "expedition," in which members of European nobility traveled in caravans with a retinue of cooks, valets, camp tenders, scouts, and artists. Now Pullman provided the caravan, the cook, and the porter.

The essay opens with a mock-disparaging statement: "Now I am conscious that all my life I have seen men who owned shotguns and setter dogs, and that these persons were wont at intervals to disappear from their usual haunts with this paraphernalia. Without thinking I felt that they went to slay little birds, and for them I entertained a goodnatured contempt" (*CW,* 160). Then, in accord with the convention of the sporting story, he marshals facts with tongue in cheek to demonstrate that this "unthinking" contempt was unwarranted. Prairie chickens are not easy quarry; they "rattle" a man when they are on the fly and are hard to hit, especially if the man is "a good shooter but a bad hitter" (*CW,* 161). A well-trained setter is a marvel at work; ducks must be "led" a good distance; wet, muddy clothing and stinging insects provide the requisite discomfort of an outing; a long day and a long, cold wagon ride back to the car build a healthy appetite for steak.

The location of this hunt is equally mundane. Their terrain is the vast, flat wheatlands of Dakota, which they must share with farmers and their threshing machines that belch black smoke. This is not the land of true sportsmen. There is nothing rigorous or even remotely dangerous. Although walking over the stubble provides good exercise, duck shooting has no action but is merely a calm, deliberate shedding of blood and a wounding of many birds. "The chicken shooting is not laborious, since one rides in a wagon, and a one-lunged wooden-legged man is as good as a four-mile athlete" (*CW,* 163).

If a man becomes a shotgun enthusiast he will discover a surprising number of fellows who are willing to go with him or to be interested in his tales. Such men, however enthusiastic, are not Remington tribesmen. Thus he was pleased to learn that the car was to be attached that night to an express train bound west, and he "crawled into the upper bunk to dream of badlands, elk, soldiers, and cowboys" (*CW,* 163).

Sporting dudes and duck shooting are given the jocular treatment again in "Winter Shooting on the Gulf Coast of Florida" (*Harper's Weekly,* 11 May 1895), a short, witty essay illustrated with a montage of sketches of Remington and fellow sports banging away at ducks from boat and shore. The sporting life of the gun-club set is succinctly described: "Ducks down there are confiding birds, and a boat loaded with girls and grub and Scotch whiskey and soda can be sailed right up to them while the sportsman empties his shotgun and fills his game-bag" (*CW,* 188). Not an activity for a tribesman.

On several occasions, Remington was invited by General Nelson Miles, one of his most revered heroes, to join him on various expeditions. One such outing was recorded in the excellent "Bear-Chasing in the Rocky Mountains" (*Harper's Monthly,* July 1895), a hunt on a ranch in New Mexico. The owner, an Englishman named Montague Stevens, presides over an immense territory. Stevens's "door-yard is some hundreds of miles of mountain wilderness and desolate mesa—a more gorgeous preserve than any king ever dreamed of possessing for his pleasure—with its plains dotted with antelope, and its mountains filled with cougar, deer, bear, and wild turkeys" (*CW,* 197).

Remington is pleased to be back in the Southwest, where he feels that he is among "his people": a rancher and his cowpunchers, and a general with his officers and troopers. Many of the group has met with violence. Stevens has lost an arm; a professional bear hunter named Cooper has recently been shot in the face; and a Captain Mickler has "led barefooted cavalrymen over these hills in pursuit of Apaches at a date in history when I was carefully conjugating Latin verbs" (*CW,* 202).

Stevens's purpose now is to hunt down an enormous grizzly that for two years has been feasting on his cattle and eluding all efforts to bring him down. Early one morning, the company sets off across the plain and into the mountains. In the lead are Dan, the ranch foreman, and Cooper, the hunter, who looks out for "bear signs." Next come Montague Stevens, with an assortment of dogs, and finally General Miles, his son, various calvarymen, and Remington himself. All this, says Remington, "made a picture, but, like all Western canvases, too big for a frame. . . . The spirit of the thing is not hunting but the chase of the bear, taking one's mind back to the buffalo, or the nobles of the Middle Ages, who made their 'image of war' with bigger game than red foxes" (*CW,* 200).

After days of hard riding, in rigorous conditions, over steep, mountainous terrain, the party splits up, Remington riding with Captain Mickler. As they make their way down a treacherous hill, they hear the dogs, then shots. A startled cavalry orderly had seen a huge silver-tip bearing down on him, chased by dogs. He had shot, but missed, and the bear had taken off down a canyon. After an hour's weary traveling, Remington and Mickler come out on the plain and there, under a tree, lies the dead silver-tip.

The conclusion is ironic. Three of Stevens's cowboys had been working in the foothills, had heard the shots, had seen the bear, and having no guns, had roped him. With noteworthy accuracy, the punchers had caught the bear's head, the paws, and the hind legs, and had tied the ropes to a tree. "The roaring, biting, clawing mass of hair was practically helpless, but to kill him was an undertaking" (*CW,* 202). They finally stuck a knife into a vital part, loaded him on a pony, and brought him in. It was a daring performance but was regarded by the punchers as a great joke.

That the bear was killed not by any of the hunters but by unarmed cowboys was the kind of anticlimactic ending that Remington found amusing. At the same time, he sees bear hunting as truly sportsmanlike. The hunter must ride into the remote country the bear inhabits, and he must be willing to confront an aggressive creature of the enormous strength of the silver-tip. The hunt led Remington to ponder on the spiritual kinship of hunter, savage, and bear. He rode back into camp, "thinking on the savagery of man. One never heard of a bear which travelled all the way from New Mexico to Chicago to kill a man, and yet a man will go 3,000 miles to kill a bear" (*CW,* 203).

The story's ending may also echo an earlier tradition. The lord and nobles chased the boar or stag. If they failed to kill by lance, when the dogs brought the quarry to bay, servants of the hunt were sent to dispatch it with axe or club or stones. In the epic, democratic West, cowboys did the job with lariats and a knife.

As Remington's income rose, he took pride in friendships with men in New York's social and professional class, and he was pleased to be identified with what Ben Vorpahl describes as "the curiosity then commonly known in genteel circles as a 'D. F.,' or 'damn fine' fellow" (Vorpahl 1978, 207). In "The Strange Days That Came to Jimmie Friday" (*Harper's Monthly,* August 1896), Remington recounts making a canoe trip into the remote Canadian wilderness in the company of two Damn Fine fellows, a journey that met his ideal of physical challenge and his glory in unspoilt nature. It also stirred him to sensitive reflection on the life of their Indian guide.

The plans began amusingly when Remington and five friends met for lunch at the fashionable Savarin restaurant in New York City, a lunch that Remington describes as "making through connections to dinner without change." Forming themselves as the "Abwee-chemun" club (Algonquin for "paddle and canoe"), they propose exploring the land of unknown lakes and unnamed rivers of northern Canada, each with a little cedar canoe. Three members cravenly back out, but in the morning, Remington and two stalwarts remain, one a lawyer who loved nature but detested canoes, the other "nominally a merchant but in reality an atavic Norseman" (*CW,* 225).

The two-week adventure begins with a night in a lumberman's hotel with houseflies and smelly beds. The three "Abwees" are told by the Hudson Bay Company factor that the lakes and rivers they seek are some days' journey into the "beyond." They find their guide in Jimmie Friday, an Indian trapper who regularly brings a toboggan load of furs into the fort every spring and sometimes served as guide for bushrangers—men who explored pine lands for great lumber firms. Having hired two French Indian voyagers and a Scotch Canadian boy as helpers, the Abwees pick up their three highly polished canoes, collect their supplies, and set off by steamboat. After two days' travel, they are put ashore on a pebbly beach, deep into the "beyond" they had sought. Much like Remington's earlier canoeing venture described in "Black Water and Shallows," the portage and camping are rough and demanding, compensated by the beauties of unspoilt nature.

Their journey begins with a long portage. Each Abwee carries his own belongings and his canoe, a test of endurance they proudly pass, dubbing themselves "dead game sports." On the river, the Scotch boy and Jimmie Friday man one large supply canoe, the two French Indians the other. "So the Abwees went down the river on a golden morning, their double-blade paddles flashing the sun and sending the drip in a shower on the glassy water. The smoke from the lawyer's pipe hung behind him in the quiet air." The Norseman calls out, "Say! this suits me. I am never going back to New York" (CW, 227). They all agree that these days in the wilderness should be "happy singing flights of time."

The river swarms with fish, enough to fill the pot in half an hour. Days of rapids and portage upstream bring them farther into "the beyond," where there is no trace of man and only Jimmie Friday knows the way, for this is his trapping ground. Remington becomes intrigued by the simple and isolated life of their guide. He learns that Jimmie suffers from tuberculosis but carries on without complaint. The pattern of Jimmie's life was set for him early. In the winter he and his brother leave his mother with cords of stove wood for the summer while he guides bushrangers and occasionally spends a few days in the lumber town before returning home with winter supplies.

On one gray day, the Abwees reach a little board dock and see a few tiny log houses—a remote outpost of the Hudson Bay Company. This is Jimmie's home. "Here we saw his poor old mother, who was being tossed about in the smallest of canoes as she drew her nets. Jimmie's father had gone out on a hunting expedition and had never come back. Some day Jimmie's old mother will go out on the wild lake to tend her nets, and she will not come back. Some time Jimmie too will not return—for the Indian struggle with nature is appalling in its fierceness" (*CW,* 231).

There is little pleasure to be found here. Remington, by nature a gregarious person, sees in this place isolated people who will die lonely deaths, weakened by hardship, meager diet, and disease. A man of intellectual energy, he is stirred by the stagnation of such a life and appalled by what the winters must be like in the tiny log cabins. From such a place, Jimmie goes to a lumber town for a taste of "civilization."

At the hacienda San Jose de Bavicora, 225 arid miles from Chihuahua, Remington had observed another outpost of civilization, but there the people of various occupations met together at the hacienda. There was a season when vaqueros went out alone with distant herds, just as Jimmie and his brother alternately walk their trap lines, but the vaquero comes back to serenades, dances, and rodeos, where friends meet friends from other ranches. Bavicora is a community with neighboring, though distant, communities. Jimmie's home is an isolated monoculture, where life is reduced to a lonely struggle with nature.

During the outing with the Abwees, Jimmie's serious mien had thawed, and he often grinned happily at their antics. For two golden weeks, three New Yorkers and four young woodsmen were carefree together. Jimmie found himself among men who were neither trapping nor lumbering, men for whom canoeing, exploring, camping, and eating were all acts of pleasure. For those two weeks he could forget the tuberculosis that would kill him, as surely as it killed Remington's father. "And thus it was that the gloomy Indian Jimmie Friday . . . was happy in these strange days—even to the extent of looking with wondrous eyes on the nooks which we loved—nooks which previously for him had only sheltered possible 'dead-falls' or not, as the discerning eye of the trapper decided the prospect for pelf" (*CW,* 227).

The journey comes to an end with the group passing through beautiful little lakes, gliding out on the big lake, and catching the steamer going to Bais des Pierres. There they hand over the remains of their provisions to Jimmie, who lays in his own winter supplies and shoves off in his boat. The Abwees watch sadly and agree that Jimmie was "a lovely Injun." Then the Norseman stands up, stamps his foot, and says, "By George, fellows, any D. F. would call this a sporting trip" (*CW,* 231).

A less triumphant outcome marked Remington's encounter with appalling cold in "The White Forest" (*Harper's Monthly,* December 1898), an account of a caribou hunt in the St. Laurentian mountains of

Canada that stretches a test of endurance to the extreme. Three men—
Remington, an old "Yale stroke," and an "Essex trooper"—elect to take
their winter outing in Quebec rather than in Florida. Ostensibly their
purpose is to hunt caribou, but their desire is to face the challenge of the
cold, "to get out on the snow—to get in the snow—to tempt its moods
and feel its impulse" (*CW,* 349). In the end, they get more than they
bargained for.

Layered in woolens and carrying bags of blankets and frozen beef,
pork, and potatoes, they go by train from Quebec to St. Raymond and
by sleigh from St. Raymond to a hunting club camp. At this first camp
they are in high spirits, stripping off their clothes, dousing each other
with cold water, and dashing back into the warm cabin, to the disgust of
the camp master. The next day, accompanied by three French Canadian
guides towing toboggans, they snowshoe to a cabin in the bush to spend
the next seven days hunting.

They are forced to return to the first camp to get snowshoes that fit
and to learn to wear layers of socks to make them bearable. They step
through snow drifts into hidden streams of freezing water. They marvel
at the French Canadians who can pull toboggans loaded with a hundred
pounds. The caribou was the color of the tree trunks among which it
lived, and they learn that its hooves are so adapted it can run in four feet
of snow with the speed of a red deer on dry ground. The deathly stillness
of the winter forest is haunting. If the hunter runs against a tree, he may
start an avalanche of snow that sounds like thunder in the silence. Remington misses his own chance at a caribou when one snowshoe sinks
slowly under him.

The only caribou they bagged was killed by one of the guides and
was set up frozen to be photographed and painted. After days of stalking, their patience gave out. They backtracked to the club camp, got
into their sleighs, and "jingled into St. Raymond by the light of the
moon" (*CW,* 354).

Remington provides the usual lighthearted opening and closing paragraphs and jokes to make light of their failure to cope with the cold, but
compared with "The Strange Days of Jimmie Friday," the tone is
somber. In "The Strange Days" the woods are green and the summer
days are golden. In "The White Forest" the winter frost means death.
Canoeing is exciting, whereas snowshoeing, even while stalking game, is
simply miserable and exhausting. Remington and his friends could not
have survived, or found enjoyment, without the French Canadian
guides, who "tucked them in" and "babied" them, corrected the prob-

lems of their snowshoes, and shared their knowledge of the woods. Remington admired these woodsmen that "generations of suffering" had produced: "The men of the pack, the paddle, snowshoe, toboggan, and axe do harder, more exhausting work than any other set of people; they are nearer to the primitive strain against the world of matter than are other men" (*CW,* 353). He had found another enthusiasm, another set of cheerful, friendly outdoor people, a bit toward the primitive, like Negro troopers, Mexican vaqueros, and mountain cowboys, who earned his admiration because they performed their challenging work and did it well.

Remington returns to the satiric mode in "The Trouble Brothers: Bill and the Wolf" (*Harper's Monthly,* November 1899), a burlesque of a society fox hunt. Colonel William Cody, the best-known plainsman, hunter, Indian fighter, and showman America had yet produced, comes to the army post at Fort Adobe to stage a wolf hunt. The officers stay up half the night planning the hunt and deciding to let the soldiers and their dogs participate along with the officers.

Ladies in carriages, sportsmen with Russian wolfhounds, officers with Scotch hounds, and foot soldiers with cur dogs all assemble for the event. The quarry is a woebegone wolf that Colonel Cody has purchased from an old plainsman and that sits behind the slats of its cage, "gazing far away across his native hills, silent and dignified as an Indian warrior in captivity" (*CW,* 394–95).

The outcome is hilarious. The wolf is turned loose. Everyone rushes forward. The cur dogs, not understanding the protocol of field sports, fall upon each other in tangles of wild fighting. The infantry men try to separate them and fall to fighting among themselves. Officers return to separate the men, and soon 150 men and their dogs are a swirling mass, thumping and pounding each other. The old wolf sits watching from a hill.

It is good comedy, with a mock-heroic allusion to Caesar's *Commentaries,* as Remington reflects that this is the way the Romans did things: Only bare legs and short swords were lacking. Again Remington mocks those who would attempt to abide by the formal rules of field sport.

"How a Trout Broke a Friendship" (*Outing,* September 1900) appeared in the magazine that had published Remington's first composition, "Coursing Rabbits on the Plains." Unlike the pieces done for *Harper's Monthly,* "Trout" is written with less care and the humor is somewhat overstated. It is also one of the relatively few articles for which he did no illustrations.

Remington, three friends who are "complete" anglers, and three French Indians are fishing on a lake. The three anglers are what Remington called "enthusiasts" in "Stubble and Slough in Dakota." The reference to Izaak Walton's *The Compleat Angler* (1653) indicates they are dedicated to the sport of proper angling. Like bird hunters with their shotguns, paraphernalia, and dogs, these fishermen have sacred dens at home with glass cases of "dainty rods" and hundreds of flies, stuffed fish, rare prints of the "forefathers of the lure," books of tall stories, and sundry other arcane items.

Out on the lake, Remington borrows an expensive Leonard rod from his friend Joel, hooks into a five-pound trout, and lands it with sheer brute force, to the consternation of Joel, who sees his rod being torturously bent. Apologies were to no avail: the "clumsy hands of a beanpole, worm-baiting, gill-yanking outcast had taken the soul out of Leonard's master piece" (*CW,* 420). The fisherman's sense of right and justice had been outraged to the breaking point. They did not even say goodbye to him at the railroad station.

Remington twits the enthusiast who takes his sport too seriously, who tries to make too much of it. Remington had a more visceral concept of sport. He was unimpressed by those who depended upon convention and arcane rules rather than skill or strength or endurance. He did not search for moral uplift or lessons in ethics from athletics or strenuous outdoor life, as did Theodore Roosevelt and some of Remington's old friends from the Art Students League: Dan Beard went on to organize the Boy Scouts of America, and Ernest Thompson Seton wrote and illustrated outdoor books for boys.

Remington's hard riding and wild canoeing, the brawling, the impetuous trips, the impatience with rules, and the companions in sport and pranks all have their parallels in the Canton boyhood, the Albany clerkship days, and the Kansas holiday ranching. The excitement and the humor, even the self-deprecation, have their parallels in his boyhood letters to family and friends. Throughout his life Remington savored experience, physical challenge, camaraderie, and the pleasures of the "strenuous" life.

Chapter Six

The Martial Spirit

While America in the 1890s was busily advocating and celebrating the strenuous life, it was also busy nurturing the martial spirit, a militant nationalism that found in war, as in sport, a force to build character, personal and national. An especially rhapsodic expression of the martial spirit, the address "The Soldier's Faith," was delivered to the graduating class of Harvard University on Memorial Day, 1895, by Oliver Wendell Holmes Jr., a thrice-wounded Civil War veteran, legal scholar, and later (1902–1932) Supreme Court justice.

The address begins with the lament that "war is out of fashion."[1] Commerce is now the great force. Men long for a society in which they may live without trouble or danger. Many think that love of country is an old wives' tale. Science has shaken religion in the minds of many. Holmes could imagine a time when there would be no conflict, but it is more likely that "as long as man dwells upon the globe, his destiny is battle." War and death are our racial heritage. He concedes that war, "when you are at it, is horrible and dull," and he hopes that it might be long before it occurs again, but men must be ready to face danger. For this reason, he rejoices at every dangerous sport. The "students at Heidelberg, with their sword-slashed faces," inspire him with sincere respect, and if once in a while, in the rough riding of the game of polo, a neck is broken, "I regard it, not as a waste, but as a price well paid for the breeding of a race fit for headship and command" (Lerner, 23). Among the lessons that he and his fellow soldiers have learned in the Civil War are "to ride boldly at what is in front of you, be it fence or enemy; to pray, not for comfort but for combat"; to love glory more than ease; and especially to believe that "love of country is not an idle name" (Lerner, 24).

Many Americans shared Holmes's sentiments. A central theme in Brooks Adams's *Law of Civilization and Decay* (1896) is that the economic mind is corrupting the artistic and martial spirits of modern society. In his preface to *The Virginian,* Owen Wister condemned alike the ethics of Wall Street and the morals of Newport society. If the cowpuncher "gave his word, he kept it; Wall Street would have found him behind the times. Nor did he talk lewdly to women; Newport would have thought him old-fashioned."[2]

Although many Americans might have shuddered at Holmes's saber-slashed Heidelbergians, they rejoiced in violent and dangerous spectator sports. By the 1890s rodeos had become Western regional events with battered bulldoggers and bronco busters in contests as breakneck as anything Remington saw in Los Ojos.[3] Professional boxing, once on a social par with the barroom brawl and still barred in many places, had become a national, million-dollar sport, and in John L. Sullivan had given Irish-Americans an ethnic hero.

Declining love of country became a popular concern. In 1892 Francis Bellamy, brother of the author of the Utopian novel *Looking Backward* (1888), composed the Pledge of Allegiance and persuaded President Harrison to call for every school to fly the national flag and to conduct patriotic exercises.[4]

A man of Remington's nature and temperament found much to his liking in the promulgation of the martial spirit. At the age of 17, in a letter discussing his future, he had written to his Uncle Horace: "There is just one obstruction between me and prosperity, that is, if Uncle Sam ever gets into any delicate controversy I will leave my bones where thousands of patriotic Americans have deposited theirs within the past fifteen years" (Splete, 22).

In his adult writings, Remington was willing to state the grim correlative to the patriotic sacrifice: The ultimate duty of the soldier was to die, his daily job was killing. In "A Day with the Seventh Regiment" (*Harper's Weekly*, 18 July 1891), an article reviewing an officer's training program at Peekskill, New York, he dismisses the belief of some that universal peace is at hand and that men who do not like fighting will convince others to the same view. Like Holmes, he believes that such a change in human nature is unlikely: "As an eccentric old fighting colonel of the regular army once said to me as we stood looking at his men, 'They need a little killing; can't have soldiers without fightin' '" (*CW*, 83).

Remington differed from Holmes in being less polemic. In all that Remington published on the subject of arms and man, there is little of God, Country, Flag, or Manifest Destiny as the mission of the English-speaking people, so often invoked in the political discourse of the 1890s. He differed as well in his view of the soldier as volunteer or professional. Holmes himself, like Remington's father, had served as a volunteer in the Civil War, leading companies of men conscripted by states.

He envisages an army of citizens fired by love of country and tempered by honest labor and hardy sport, who learned lessons of war in combat. Holmes sees them returning, after their tour of duty is done, imbued with the soldier's virtues, ready to give counsel to the young, who will in turn some day answer the call. Remington, on the other hand, while not disparaging his father's volunteer service, had come to know and praise the regular army that had fought war after war with the Indian nations, and in between had protected Indians and cowboys and settlers from each other, an army of men who had chosen soldiering as their vocation and whose virtues were competence, dependability, endurance, and pride in self and company. It was a difference in point of view that affected Remington's portrayal of the Cuban campaign when war came. Roosevelt's Rough Riders were volunteers, stealing much of the glory from the professional soldiers who did the basic fighting.

Remington feared that with the pacification of the frontier, America would become indifferent to the welfare of the army (a fear shared with the army) and that the spirit of the fighting man would decline. Between 1891 and the summer of 1898, he wrote and illustrated many accounts of army training programs, tactics, field exercises, and new military equipment, all intended to keep alive the public's interest in the military. He worried that civilians might not understand or appreciate the rough soldier.

In the seriocomic piece "With the Guns" (*Harper's Weekly,* 17 August 1895), Remington makes humor out of "civilian misapprehension." He accompanies an artillery battery as it goes on a march in the Berkshires, proceeding from Fort Hamilton, down New York Bay. Along the way they are received by the townspeople with gusto, but in Massachusetts many good people were slightly alarmed by the prospect of regular soldiers among them. Perhaps they recalled the British occupation or possibly the reckless homecoming of the volunteers of '65, but soon their fears begin to allay, and many come to the captain to say they are gratified that his men are a decent lot of young chaps. The "bronzed and rugged old soldier" cannot comprehend why the civilians do not understand that the soldier, "so much dreaded by the smug civilian, is a happy-go-lucky fellow, better natured than his money-hunting brother," and that he has been "killed by the hundreds" for the benefit of this "smug 'cit' " (*CW,* 213).

The soldiers patiently answer many foolish questions about the guns and are particularly nice to the young ladies. Brass bands play, and visions of old days pass through the fancies of old Civil War veterans.

The people give the men refreshments and make officers honorary members of clubs. During this fraternizing, Remington is swapping yarns with old soldiers, veterans of the Southwest Indian wars. The article is a lighthearted contribution to Remington's efforts to create favorable images of the military.

There is much in Remington's rugged soldier that resembles Rudyard Kipling's Tommy Atkins. In 1895, when Kipling was living in the United States, he and Remington had become occasional drinking and debating companions at the Players Club in Manhattan. By 1897 Theodore Roosevelt, who knew both men, wrote to Remington: "I don't know how you do it, any more than I know how Kipling does it; but somehow you get close not only to the plainsman and soldier, but to the half-breed and Indian, in the same way Kipling does to the British Tommy and the Gloucester codfisher" (Splete, 288). Like Kipling, Remington wanted his soldier to be realistic, not idealized. Asked to illustrate an article by Lieutenant Alvin Sydenham, titled "Tommy Atkins in the American Army" (*Harper's Weekly,* 13 August 1892), Remington wrote to Sydenham, urging him to describe more details of the soldier and "tell how he acts and talks and eats and fights and swears and even makes love" (Splete, 137). He agreed with Kipling that "[s]ingle men in barracks don't grow into plaster saints."

Training exercises and new equipment were not enough to keep the soldier trim and spirited. In what today seems a rather appalling statement, he writes that it would be wise to "keep a little of the military seed corn in a country, if only for your mobs, which 'ye have always with you.' " In the absence of war, the "mobs" might be useful in filling the need for a little killing (*CW,* 83).

In the summer of 1894 the opportunity came in the Pullman strike in Chicago, and for a few days Remington became a combat correspondent again. In the midst of a depression, the Pullman Company had reduced employee wages without reducing rents in company housing, touching off a boycott that affected national rail transportation. President Cleveland sent General Miles to restore order, and Remington covered the event for *Harper's Weekly,* reporting the military occupation in three articles: "Chicago under the Mob" (21 July), "Chicago under the Law" (21 July), and "The Withdrawal of the U.S. Troops" (11 August). Remington's sympathies were entirely on the side of law and order. In his opinion—along with that of General Miles, the "better" people of Chicago, and most of the national press—the governor of Illinois, the mayor of Chicago, and the local police had given the city over to loafers and anarchists from the "Central European peasantry here in Chicago" (*CW,* 155), and so Chicago had to be saved from itself. General Miles had amassed a small army from various regiments of the Western command. Acting with restraint in the face of insults and threats—as they saw it—the army held the city in order until the strike ended, then withdrew out of Chicago and its "hostile population" to Fort Sheridan, into "the United States of America proper," where they were saluted by "the waving of flags and cheers" (*CW,* 165).

All the elements of Remington's martial vision are present: the Indian-fighting army with its old friends; the hard-working, ill-fed American trooper versus the alien striker who will not work or let others work who want to; the temporizing citizen and politician who scorn the simple fighting soldier until the soldier comes to the rescue. Then, as Kipling puts it, "It's thank you, Mr. Atkins, when the bands begin to play."

With all this, however, Remington was disappointed. The Pullman strike was not the martial equivalent of war. The soldiers had been forced to restrain their natural function of killing the enemy. He complains that "statesmen fail to understand that soldiers are not police, and that police work deteriorates troops. They never study law or how to be diplomatically nice on occasion. Soldiers only know their trade—that's fighting. They should never be made to associate with a mob, except after their manner, which is to get strategically near enough and then shoot" (*CW,* 154).

To compensate for the lack of military action in the Pullman affair, Remington decided to create a fictional version of the strike more to his liking. As Ben Merchant Vorpahl puts it, Remington created "his imagined version of what might have happened at Chicago if the mobs had truly been the insurgents he associated them with and if the Army had been freed of all restraints" (Vorpahl 1978, 171). Remington's fantasy, "The Affair of the ___th of July" (*Harper's Weekly,* 2 February 1895), purports to be a letter written by a young military aide-de-camp named Jack to "a friend." As the story begins, the Chicago police force has been demoralized and martial law has been proclaimed. Factories and stores have been closed and troopers are sharing their rations with honest citizens. The "turbulent elements" have organized against the federal authority. Both sides are armed, and there is plenty of killing. Jack sees artillerymen sweeping the streets with cannon fire and Gatling guns, soldiers wounded and killed by dynamite at an infantry camp, hospital tents ablaze with lanterns where doctors are already at their gruesome

work, a building occupied by strikers set ablaze with requisitioned
kerosene, and a fierce battle inside the railroad depot. Some of the mob
move out into the residential area to loot. Jack saves the life of a
sergeant and rescues a young lady from looters who are drinking up the
family champagne. The next day the army executes hundreds of prisoners, piles them on flatcars "like cordwood," and buries them out in the
country somewhere. In the end, Jack's letter confesses that "all this
never really happened, but it all might very easily have happened if the
mob had continued to monkey with the military buzz-saw" (*CW,* 183).

How much this excessive blood lust expressed by Remington was
genuine is a question. Peggy and Harold Samuels give the following
commentary in their "Notes" for the *Collected Writings:* "The senior
Harper's illustrator W. A. Rogers wrote in his autobiography that a
stranger meeting Remington would come away with the impression
that he had met a man of blood and iron. Rogers felt it was the pic-
turesqueness of battles that misled Remington into an imaginary love
for kill and be killed, blood and more blood, whereas Remington was
really a big overgrown boy, full of the charm of make-believe"
(*CW,* 604).

Whatever divided feelings he may have had, it is certain that Remington eagerly looked for a war. In 1891 he had hoped that there might
be war between Russia and Germany that he and Poultney Bigelow
might cover. In 1893 he was miffed that *Harper's* would not send him to
Morocco, where there was some "d--- good fighting going on" (Samuels,
197). In 1894, in a letter to Bigelow, he even considered covering the
"turn up" between China and Japan but could not imagine making
"those apes seem like real soldiers" (Splete, 211).

Hope for a war with Spain rested upon the insurgency in Cuba, for
which there was considerable emotional, and some material, support,
such as the abortive December 1896 filibustering expedition that gave
Stephen Crane the shipwreck experience for his short story "The Open
Boat" (1897). Remington was encouraged when William Randolph
Hearst sent him to Cuba, along with Richard Harding Davis, to meet
secretly with the insurgents' leader, General Gómez. The trip began
with comic-opera derring-do and a near shipwreck and dwindled off
into a tour by railroad, limited to the area controlled by the Spanish.
They never reached General Gómez. The trip is mostly noted for its
contribution to the folklore of journalism, the tale that Remington
cabled Hearst that there was no war, to which Hearst replied, "You furnish the pictures and I'll furnish the war."[5] Remington left Cuba, while

Davis stayed on to send dispatches for Remington to illustrate. Remington was already home when a full front-page article in Hearst's *New York Journal* (27 January 1897) announced that Davis and Remington were in Cuba for the *Journal,* had reached the insurgents (which they had not), and would be presenting a true account of the situation in Cuba. Some of the text and illustrations carried the message that Hearst and the *Journal* wanted: Spanish soldiers murdering wounded Cubans, Spanish firing squads executing Cuban patriots, Spanish guerrillas cruelly mistreating a captured man and woman. The propaganda also gave the impression of an ill-equipped, poorly led, undernourished Spanish army that could be quickly defeated by any modern army with the will to do so.

Still, there was little public enthusiasm for a war with Spain until February 1898, when the sinking of the battleship *Maine* in Havana harbor, with the loss of American lives, incited patriotic fervor. Even so, it was April 1898 before war was declared.

Volunteer regiments sprang up all over the country. By mid-April Congress had passed a bill providing for "three regiments from the wild riders and riflemen of the Rockies and Great Plains."[6] There was little doubt in these cowboys' minds that they were sufficiently trained in horsemanship, although they did not have the army training that Remington regarded as essential.

Remington was engaged as war correspondent by both *Harper's* and Hearst. While the blockade was in force against Cuba, he joined the gathering of forces in Tampa, Florida, in what Richard Harding Davis called the "rocking-chair" period of the war, which took place on the porch of the Tampa Bay Hotel. The first war article Remington sent to *Harper's* was "The War Dreams" (*Harper's Weekly,* 7 May 1898), a brief, humorous account of a hotel banquet where four officers tell the bizarre dreams they had the night before. When there is no action, he implies, only trivia can be reported.

The second article, "Wigwags from the Blockade" (*Harper's Weekly,* 14 May 1898), is Remington's impression of six days he spent on the battleship *Iowa.* Impatient at the inactivity, he explores the ship but doesn't take to the navy, with its machinery and technology. The men seem to him to "have succumbed to modern science" (*CW,* 305). His heart is with the cavalry horse, the saber, and the rifle, not with modern science that turns fighting men into tenders of machines.

Remington was popular with the rocking-chair army officers, and he enjoyed being with the troopers of his first love, the Ninth U.S. Cavalry

(Colored). In "Soldiers Who Cry" (*Harper's Weekly,* 24 May 1898), Remington recounts what he heard from Colonel Powell of the Ninth Infantry: When the regiment left its post in New York, the old colonel ordered details out of each regiment to stay behind to look after government property. When he dismissed the men, they stood there "crying, blubbering, and beseeching Colonel Powell not to make them stay behind." Proudly, Remington declares, "That is the kind of boys to follow the band, I say" (*CW,* 308).

At last the waiting was over. On 22 June he and the other correspondents accompanying the troops landed at Daiquirí on the southwest coast of Cuba. Remington's article about the Santiago campaign, "With the Fifth Corps" (*Harper's Monthly,* November 1898), is an outstanding piece of personal journalism that chronicles the events he observed and the disillusion he suffered.

The first paragraph begins in a light tone but ends in a statement that constitutes Remington's credo for all soldiers and correspondents: "I approach this subject of the Santiago campaign with awe, since the ablest correspondents in the country were all there, and they wore out lead pencils most industriously. I know I cannot add to the facts, but I remember my own emotions, which were numerous, interesting, and, on the whole, not pleasant. I am as yet unable to decide whether sleeping in a mud-puddle, the confinement of a troopship, or being shot at is the worst. . . . However, they satisfied a life of longing to see men do the greatest thing which men are called on to do" (*CW,* 338). At last he has found a real war, where men will face their noblest sacrifice.

From the first everything went wrong. Remington is outraged to learn that the cavalry has been dismounted, his beloved cavalry reduced to the role of foot soldiers. Cuba is hot, wet, and steaming, a far cry from the dry Southwest or the cold northern plains. When they disembark, Remington tarries with the Sixth Cavalry (the old "Galloping Sixth") and thus misses the action at Las Guásimas, where Theodore Roosevelt and his Rough Riders make a successful skirmish. Determined not to be caught again, he and John Fox Jr. leave the protection of the general's camp and set off on their own to stay near the front.[7]

Then all the forward movement comes to a halt while the army builds bridges and roads. "The men were on half-rations, were out of tobacco, and it rained, rained, rained. We were very miserable" (*CW,* 343). He and Fox were without even a pup tent for shelter, sleeping on ponchos in a sea of mud. Fox was worried that he was "subject to malaria." Remington fears that "this cold of mine will end in congestion of the lungs." When asked for a remedy, Fox suggests the best remedy is the "fare to New York" (*CW,* 343). Remington purchases a horse, for which he says he is "ostracized" by his fellow correspondents.[8] Impatiently they hear the rumors that the forward movement will come, and at last, after several days, they hear the sounds of battle. Remington steals a feed of oats for his horse, remarking on the "demoralizing" effect of war, and rides forth to find the action.

Following a staff officer, Remington rides toward the stone fort at Caney, coming to a hill where they can see the battery below. Now he sees that the battery, with its smoky guns, is showing the Spanish shrapnel where to fire and learns that smoky guns are outdated. "All this time no one's glass could locate the fire of the Spanish guns, and we could see Capron's smoke miles away on our right" (*CW,* 344). He goes far up the hill, "walking over the prostrate bodies of my old friends, the Tenth Cavalry, who were hugging the hot ground to get away from the hotter shrapnel" (*CW,* 344). At the top of the hill he meets with a "clubmate from New York, and sundry good foreigners . . . and listened to much expert artillery talk, though the talk was not quite so impressive as the practice of that art" (*CW,* 344). Clearly artillery was not performing as expected.

He leaves the talk of military science to go down to the road where the human beings are who "do these things." The jungle road is crowded with soldiers standing or lying or moving slowly forward. He winds his way along with them, saying, "Gangway, please."

Now, he pauses in the essay to reflect on his state of mind: "War is productive of so many results, things happen so awfully fast, men do such strange things, pictures make themselves at every turn, the emotions are so tremendously strained, that what knowledge I had fled away from my brain, and I was in a trance; and do you know, cheerful reader, I am not going to describe a battle to you" (*CW,* 344). Instead of a traditional formal account of a battle, he will convey a mélange of sounds and "pictures" and bits of emotion and "knowledge." The Spanish Mauser bullets flying through the trees "make noises such as you can make if you strike quickly with a small walking stick at a few very green leaves" (*CW,* 344). At the field hospital at the ford of the San Juan River, "a man came, stooping over, with his arms drawn up; and hands slapping down at the wrists. This is the way with all people when they are shot through the body, because they want to hold the torso steady, because if they don't it hurts" (*CW,* 345). Nearby a squad of men "scrape and whittle away" trying to fix a "dynamite gun" while the "bullets come like rain" and the gunnery mules and horses "lay down one after another" (*CW,* 345). "It made my nerves jump, looking at that gruesome hospital, sand-covered, with bleeding men, and yet it seemed to have fascinated me; but I gathered myself and stole away" (*CW,* 346). Remington did not see the famous charge of San Juan Hill, but he did see its end. He had his first glimpse of San Juan Hill from a small bank, while bullets whistled about him. He crawled to a new place and through glasses he "finally got a sight of the fort, and just then I could distinguish our blue soldiers on the hilltop, and I also noticed that the Mauser bullets rained no more. Then I started after. The country was alive with wounded men—some to die in the dreary jungle, some to get their happy-home draft, but all to be miserable. Only a handful of men got to the top, where they broke out a flag and cheered" (*CW,* 346). Remington had glimpsed the scene that would reign supreme in patriotic images until the flag was raised on Iwo Jima in World War II.[9] Richard Harding Davis added a cavalry flag and gave a more stirring description of it to end his account of the Battle of San Juan Hill.[10] But the battle had not ended. Remington followed troops up to the top of the hill where "our men sat about in little bunches in the pea-green guinea-grass, exhausted. A young officer of the Twenty-Fourth, who was very much excited, threw his arms about me, and pointing to twenty-five big negro infantrymen sitting near, said, 'That's all—that is all that is left of the 24th Infantry,' and the tears ran off his mustache" (*CW,* 346–47). The Spanish trenches were full of dead; they were "horrible." Now the Spanish were trying to retake the hill. The air was crowded with flying bullets and screaming shrapnel. The effort failed, but Remington had had enough. He helped a wounded man back to the field hospital, and now, for the first time in the article, he admits to the gravity of his own physical condition. "I found I was too weak myself to walk far. I had been ill during the whole campaign, and latterly had fever, which, taken together with the heat, sleeping in the mud, marching, and insufficient food, had done for me" (*CW,* 348).

As he made his way through the rear of the battle, he was shaken by what he saw. "All the broken spirits, bloody bodies, hopeless, helpless suffering which drags its dreary length to the rear, are so much more appalling than anything else in the world that words won't mean anything to one who has not seen it. Men half naked, men sitting down on the road-side utterly spent, men hopping on one foot with a rifle for a crutch, men out of their minds from sunstroke, men dead and men dying" (*CW,* 348).

The next day, he tries to return to the front but gives it up, recognizing that, in the last word of the article, he is "finished." He booked passage on a ship and returned to New York.

The Santiago campaign was a sobering experience; out of it he produced what Peggy and Harold Samuels aptly call "a dispassionate description of the kind of men he now understood, the men who did their prudent best, waiting out enemy salvos behind a river bank and advancing by crawling on their knees" (Samuels, 187). It was not the kind of war he had envisioned, with noble cavalry charges on horseback against a heroic foe. Modern warfare was ugly and brutal.

Remington received high praise for the article. C. C. Buel, an editor of *Century* magazine, wrote to Remington 28 October 1898 that he wanted to thank him for "leaving your fellows of the quill so far behind" and "outdoing everybody with a description of the scenes and emotions of that remarkable advance to San Juan" (Splete, 232). Even Emerson Hough, a writer of historical fiction who was not ordinarily an admirer of Remington, is quoted as saying, "When all the country was palpitating with high-geared war stories, the best war story written was by Frederic Remington" (*CW,* 617).

The Santiago campaign had its political significance, especially for Theodore Roosevelt. The Rough Riders had caught, and nourished, the attention of the press. Roosevelt began campaigning for the governorship of New York soon after the flag was planted on San Juan Hill, and his service with the Rough Riders was to be the central theme of his campaign. In his outwardly friendly relationship with Roosevelt, Remington had often found him patronizing, and in Cuba he had not been invited by Roosevelt to accompany him during the fighting. In his essay, Remington downplays the role of the Rough Riders, emphasizing the role of the regular army throughout the campaign. He wants to set the record straight that the role of the volunteers has been overemphasized. He baldly states that "San Juan was taken by infantry of the United States regular army without the aid of artillery. It was the most glorious feat of arms I ever heard of, considering every condition" (*CW,* 346). These are the soldiers who do their stalwart best. These are the men who will be there when the volunteers go home.

The illustrations that Remington did for "With the Fifth Corps" show his focus on soldiers under shrapnel fire, on horses and men silently picked off, on soldiers wounded and dying. These are the subjects that were of first interest to him, as opposed to traditional battle scenes. After the war, he turned down many requests for illustrating or

writing about the Cuban campaign, but those items he did do empha-
sized the same subjects. In "They Bore a Hand" (*Harper's Monthly,* April
1900), the old soldier at San Juan takes his major back down "to the
blood-soaked sands beside the river, where the surgeons were working
grimly and quickly." These were the scenes that haunted Remington,
that stayed in his mind, that destroyed his illusions of the glory of war.

Although his relations with Roosevelt were not cordial during the
war, their friendship was renewed soon afterward when Roosevelt's
Rough Riders gave him a bronze of Remington's *The Bronco Buster,* occa-
sioning a warm exchange of letters between the two men. Then Roosevelt, while writing "The Cavalry at Santiago" for Scribner's, urged
Remington to do an illustration for him. Remington was reluctant,
declaring he had not seen the actual event, but Roosevelt prevailed, and
the now-famous painting *Charge of the Rough Riders at San Juan Hill*
appeared in April 1899. In the center of the painting, among the soldiers, Remington included a Negro trooper, perhaps to negate Roosevelt's implication, in the article, that Negro soldiers were inclined to
drift toward the rear unless led by white officers.

The painting became a source of irritation to Remington for some
years. Roosevelt's political enemies initiated a continuing controversy,
described by Peggy and Harold Samuels: "There were witnesses to
swear that Roosevelt had been on foot during the charge, not mounted,
and that the Rough Riders had charged Kettle Hill on San Juan heights,
not San Juan Hill itself. Remington who had missed seeing the actual
charge was caught in the middle. He was still defending his subject
matter against the New York Sun a decade later, and when he listed the
162 paintings in color that he considered to be worth calling fine art, he
did not include the 'Charge of the Rough Riders at San Juan Hill' "
(Samuels, 291–92).

Except for two brief articles about Cuba after the war for *Collier's*
magazine, Remington had little else to add. "Havana under Our Regulars" (April 1999) and "Cuban Bandits in Santiago Province" (22 April
1899) praise the peacekeeping regular army soldiers who maintain
order, just as they had done in the Southwest and the plains of the
Indian wars.

The Cuban campaign had forced Remington to face the grim realities
of modern warfare. It had dampened his martial spirit but not his admiration for the common soldier.

Chapter Seven

John Ermine of the Yellowstone

While Remington was waiting for William Randolph Hearst to purchase a magazine and publish serially his novel *The Way of an Indian* (1905 – 6), he wrote his second and last novel, *John Ermine of the Yellowstone,* published by Macmillan in 1902. Both novels were set in the aftermath of Custer's last stand on the Little Big Horn River. The first was the chronicle of a Cheyenne warrior, the second a romance of a white boy raised by Indians.

The story of John Ermine begins at Virginia City, Montana, in 1804. The miners and townspeople learn that a white boy is being raised in a Crow Indian village and ride forth to rescue him. In the night his Indian foster mother steals him back, and the whole village picks up and leaves the area. White Weasel, as he is called by the Indians, is a fair-skinned, golden-haired boy, the leader of the other boys in games and pranks. When he grows to adolescence he earns his "medicine" by protecting his father's horses from the wolves. At about the age of 15, he is taken to visit an old hunchbacked white man, a hermit named Crooked Bear, whom the Crows regard as their prophet. For four years, with occasional visits to his foster parents, he lives with Crooked Bear, who teaches him English and tells him of the many marvels of the white man's world. Crooked Bear gives him the name John Ermine and sends him forth to become a scout with the white soldiers fighting the Sioux and Cheyennes. He is accompanied by a half-breed named Wolf-Voice, based on a scout that Remington had known in the past. On the journey, Ermine finds a photograph of a young woman whose features so fascinate him that he puts it in his medicine bag and carries it with him. He joins the troops in the Yellowstone Territory, proves himself a good soldier, and earns the respect of the officers and his fellow scouts. After a year of soldiering, he is stationed at a cantonment on the Yellowstone River, where he meets Katherine, the daughter of Major Searles, recognizes her as the girl in the photograph, and falls madly in love with her. With his long golden hair and beaded buckskins, he is a handsome figure. Katherine flirts with him, along with other young soldiers, but Ermine, having no knowledge of white man's social customs, misunder-

JOHN ERMINE, ILLUSTRATION BY FREDERIC REMINGTON (1902)
Photoengraving Courtesy Peggy and Harold Samuels.

stands and proposes marriage to her, not knowing she is about to become engaged to a Captain Butler. He regards the captain as his enemy; the two men quarrel, guns are drawn, and Ermine wounds Butler in the arm. He escapes, then returns, determined to kill his rival, but ironically Ermine is killed by a vengeful Indian whom he had insulted.

In writing *John Ermine* Remington was attempting something he had not done before. *The Way of an Indian* had been a straightforward narrative of the life of its Indian hero. Now Remington wanted to write a book-length novel with an integrated plot and a romance. In 1901, according to the recollections of a friend, Martha Summerhayes, he had decided "to try his hand at a novel, a real romance . . . about a little Indian boy" (*CW,* 622).[1] The little "Indian" boy soon became a white boy raised by the Indians, because Remington wanted the story to dramatize the clash of two incompatible cultures. In 1902 he was galvanized into action by the publication of two other novels early that year: Hamlin Garland's *The Captain of the Gray-Horse Troop* and Owen Wister's *The Virginian.* Remington had long argued with Garland on the subject of Indians, and he was familiar with *The Virginian* from the illustrations he had done for some of the stories that were patched together to make the novel. He regarded both works as basically unrealistic—the one for its "Noble Savage" Indian, the other for its "cowboy without cows" (Samuels, 329). He was also spurred by the competition, especially with Wister's book, which was already enormously popular.

In June he retired to Ingleneuk to write his novel, and wasted no time. By mid-September the book and illustrations were completed; by mid-November it was published. It is clear that Remington wanted to avoid the sentimentality he saw in Wister's novel. Both in his art and his writing, his goal was essentially realistic. In the encounter between the white and the Indian cultures, the Indian is inevitably on the losing side. In *The Way of an Indian,* the focus was entirely on the Indian's life, showing both its violence and its courage, ending in the Indian's tragic demise at the hands of the dominant civilization. In *John Ermine* Remington shows both sides of the coin. In childhood the protagonist learns the Indian lore of the Crows, and his long apprenticeship with the hermit Crooked Bear teaches him the advantages of civilization. The essential question becomes which of the two will prevail when both are present in the same individual and he faces a crisis for which he is not prepared.

Throughout *John Ermine* Remington emphasizes the contrasts in the two cultures and the conflict they create for his hero. As an Indian boy,

White Weasel must earn his "medicine" through some act or achievement, a vital part of Indian culture. His medicine comes to him in a
boyhood adventure. When he is old enough to spring on a horse, he is
assigned the youth's work of tending his father's horses. One day the
horse herd is attacked by wolves. The horses form a circle with White
Weasel in the center, and they fight off the wolves until they are rescued
in the morning. For this courageous act, White Weasel receives his medicine—the hoof of a white stallion that had fought for him unto death.
Remington uses an illustration in the novel similar to one he had done
for an early essay, "Horses of the Plains" (*Century,* January 1889), showing horses in a closed circle with hind legs kicking at encircling wolves.
White Weasel's foster father tells him he must always carry the hoof in
his medicine bag.

In *The Way of an Indian,* the magic of his "brown bat" protects the
hero throughout his life until the end, when it is left behind and he dies.
The conflict in the two cultures comes for young Ermine when he tells
Crooked Bear that his Indian "medicine" brought him the good fortune
of owning a gun, and his white teacher corrects him: It was the medicine of the white man that brought him the gun because " 'the Great
Spirit knew you were a white boy. The medicine of the white man is not
carried in a buckskin bag. It is carried here.' And the prophet laid his
finger on his own rather imposing brow" (*CW,* 476). Nevertheless,
Ermine later rubs his medicine on the hoofs of his pony, knowing that
Crooked Bear was probably right but half-believing that his Indian
medicine might also have some magic. It is in his medicine bag that
Ermine carries the object that he treasures: the picture of Katherine
Searles he had found on the trail.

When the Crow elders leave young White Weasel with the old man
of the mountains, the original intent is that he will be taught "the great
mysteries of the white man, together with that of the people of his own
tribe" (*CW,* 473), to prepare him so that the tribe can lean upon him in
the day when the white man comes. As Crooked Bear grows fond of the
boy, his intent changes into a desire to see that the boy has the happiness
that had been denied to himself. Because of his crooked back, he could
not be a soldier; because of his crooked back, he could not have the
woman he loved. Instead of preparing White Weasel to inherit Crooked
Bear's function as the prophet of the Crow tribe, he fills his head with
visions of glory. Now he wants him to join the white soldiers, to become
a great chief with "many wagons of coffee and sugar," and to marry a
beautiful white woman. His teachings are designed to have a "humaniz-

ing" influence on the boy, to dispel the harsh violence of the Indian world.

Until the fatal meeting with Katherine, John Ermine had made a successful entry into the world of the white man. As scouts, he and Wolf-Voice had taken part in military action and Ermine had earned a reputation for courage and reliability, qualities entirely in accord with his Indian background. His bewilderment at the flood of emotion he experiences in Katherine's presence finds him totally unprepared.

From the beginning Ermine is lost in the badinage of flirtation the others take for granted. Setting off on a wolf hunt, Katherine is surrounded by admiring young men who understand the unspoken rules of the game, while Ermine regards her every utterance as serious. She laughingly gives him her glove, which he treasures. When she says she "must have a wolf," he captures one and brings it to her door, puzzled by the merriment this causes. The word *Love* was not in his vocabulary. He had known the "easy familiarity of the Indian squaws, but none had ever stirred him. . . . The prophet had utterly neglected the boy's emotions in the interest of his intellect. The intense poverty of his experience left him without any understanding of the most ordinary conventions or casual affairs of white men's lives" (*CW,* 527).

In his emotional turmoil, Ermine behaves erratically. At Katherine's request, Ermine and Lieutenant Butler take her to visit the Indian camp. She is alarmed at the Indians' "fearful-looking faces," and Ermine sharply rebukes a young Indian who approaches them. "Go back, you brown son of mules; this squaw is my friend; I tell you she is afraid of you" (*CW,* 511). Afterward, Ermine knows that the insult to the Indian means a confrontation with him, for the Indian never forgets and always seeks his revenge.

Ermine's passion for the girl becomes obsessive. "He lay on the blanket while his thoughts alternately fevered and chilled his brain. So intense were his emotions that they did more than disorder his mind; they took smart hold of his very body, gnawing and constricting his vitals until he groaned aloud" (*CW,* 514).

On a second hunt, Katherine falls from her horse, and Ermine carries her to the edge of the stream, splashing her with water. Holding her unconscious body in his arms, he kisses her, and in this moment of high passion, he calls out, "God—God—Sak-a-war-te!" The Indian god has not been supplanted by Crooked Bear's Christian one.

Ermine's proposal of marriage to Katherine exposes all the incongruities of his divided sensibility. In one sense, he knows it is a daring move, but he understands neither the social inequality between them nor the crucial need for mutual love. Startled, she wonders how he came to entertain the idea, and he solemnly shows her the photograph he had found. "Sak-a-war-te sent it to me in the night, and he made it talk to me and he made me swear that I would seek the woman until I found her. Then she would be my wife" (*CW,* 533). As further inducement, he offers the gold mine that Crooked Bear has bequeathed to him.

Now she tries to explain that love from one side is not enough. The character of Katherine has sometimes been dismissed as an empty-headed flirt, but to Remington's credit, she is given more substance than that implies. When she sees the depth of Ermine's feelings, she speaks gently to him. She says that some mistake has occurred and she is sorry for the misunderstanding. "I simply admired you, Mr. Ermine, as I do many of the brave men about here." She would like to have a gold mine, but not unless their love was mutual. She tells him that there are other young women out in the world and that he will surely find one to his liking. But Ermine is no longer listening. He tries to answer, and "his voice dropped until she could distinguish only wild gutturals. He was talking to himself in the Indian language" (*CW,* 534).

After wounding Lieutenant Butler, Ermine flees from the camp, reflecting bitterly on the weakness that his infatuation had brought: "If I had followed my Indian heart, I could have stolen that girl out from under the noses of those soldiers . . . and rawhided her on to her horse . . . but when she looked at me, my blood turned to water" (*CW,* 540).

Remington had written about such an Indian in "Massai's Crooked Trail" (*Harper's Monthly,* January 1898), but Massai was a savage Apache who raped and discarded women. Such was not the way of the Crow or the Cheyenne. If they rode off with women, it was with their consent. The young hero of *The Way of an Indian* eloped with his first squaw, and Sun-Down Leflare once made off with the wife of an Indian chief, but both ladies were more than willing to be abducted.

John Ermine flees to his mentor, Crooked Bear, but he cannot accept the white man's advice against his vow to return and kill Butler. The Indian lust for revenge prevails and is ironically turned against him when the Indian whom he had insulted takes his own revenge, killing Ermine before he reaches Butler.

Owen Wister had given the traditional "happy ending" to *The Virginian,* but Remington scorned such weakness and maintained realism by refusing to do the same in *John Ermine.* His attorney, George M. Wright, wrote a letter addressed to "John Ermine Esq" praising this decision.

"You are all right and got yourself properly killed. I was afraid something would turn up to make you appear as a gentlemanly cowboy who should marry Katherine—but thank Heaven you respected the proprieties and died with your boots on—with your half-savage breast all untamed" (Samuels, 355).

John Seelye sees the pattern of white domination in *John Ermine* continuing from the preceding works, *The Way of an Indian* and *Sun-Down Leflare*. "In his last and most ambitious novel, Remington brought his tragic diagram to a close, for the European heritage of his young hero does not save him from the common fate of the Indians who have reared him" (Seelye, 248).

Although the principal theme of *John Ermine* is the inevitable decline of the Indian culture at the hands of the white man, it may also be seen as a part of the pattern of East versus West. Fred Erisman finds the novel notable for its reinterpretation of familiar Remington material. "*John Ermine* stands alone among Remington's books. In it, he works with familiar materials—the West, the Indians, the military—but he molds them into a tellingly different pattern. . . . Where once he found in the West unlimited opportunity for the individual to live with direct and open dealings, he now finds arbitrary, unfeeling, and institutionalized restrictions. No longer does the West judge a person's life on the basis of his achievements; instead, it judges by standards imposed from the outside. The result is tragedy, a far different result from the idyllic ending of *The Virginian*."[2]

Ben Merchant Vorpahl defines the themes in a comparison of *The Virginian* and *John Ermine:* "Wedding Molly Wood to the Virginian was a way to accomplish a truce between North and South, East and West, old and new. Katherine Searles's refusal of John Ermine was Remington's way of showing that no truce was possible between East and West, past and present, natural and civilized" (Vorpahl 1972, 14).

Criticism of *John Ermine* has generally focused on theme and historical content, sometimes with the implication that the literary quality is not equal to the thematic task. The prefatory note to the Gregg Press 1968 reprint of the novel states quite plainly, "The value of this novel lies not in its literary qualities, but in its depiction of life among the Indians and in the camps of the U.S. Cavalry, scenes which the author witnessed himself."[3] Seelye concludes that *John Ermine* "most particularly is a work whose symbolic reach far exceeds the melodramatic plot that sustains it" (Seelye, 256). In a contemporary review in the January 1903 issue of *The Reader,* Herbert Craly wrote that Remington used a method "as carefully finished as that which produced his best figures in bronze. But it takes more than the companionship of white men to make John Ermine feel at home among his own people; it takes the love of a white woman. Just here Remington visibly flinches in the illustrating, as well as in the telling of his story. And in working out his culmination, Mr. Remington's method or his patience fails him. His ending is pathetic, but it is nothing more" (*CW,* 624).

Whether the ending was true "tragedy" or mere "pathos," any assessment of the literary quality of the writing must take into account that Remington's most powerful aesthetic talent was in his art. Writing had come to him first as journalism. He never thought of himself as a "proper" writer. Even the haste with which he produced the novel was a matter of priorities: He was rushing to get back to the foundry and supervise work on his bronze *Coming through the Rye.* There are plot contrivances in the book, such as the gold mine that conveniently supplies the hermit's needs or the hackneyed device of finding the photograph of Katherine and then meeting her. In the scenes with Katherine and her parents, the dialogue is often stilted and unconvincing. But against these are the fine depictions of the Indians and the soldiers and the creation of a memorable character in John Ermine himself.

The historical setting of *John Ermine* is shared by that of *The Way of an Indian* and "How Order 6 Went Through, as Told by Sun-Down Leflare" (*Harper's Monthly,* May 1898). All three are set in the Yellowstone country in the fall and winter of 1876–1877. This is the country Remington traveled in 1890, when he went west to draw the Blackfoot Indians and had long talks with a half-breed guide and interpreter whom he named "Sun-Down Leflare" in his fiction; when he rode with General Miles's Peace Commission along the route of the battles of 1876 and '77; and when he rode with Lieutenant Casey's Cheyenne irregulars at the time of Wounded Knee, in the company of Wolf-Voice, the scout who appears in *John Ermine.* In 1876 the Crow were helping the army fight their traditional enemies, the Sioux and the Cheyennes. Two events are common to all three works: the Battle of the Little Big Horn, on 25 June 1876, where Custer and 215 men of the Seventh Cavalry were killed, and the U.S. Army's attack against the Sioux and Cheyennes that followed Custer's defeat.

In *The Way* the two great battles are seen from the Indian's point of view. In *John Ermine,* Crooked Bear, the white hermit, hears of the great battle of 1876 and soon afterward sends the 20-year-old Ermine off to join the U.S. forces to fight against the Sioux and Cheyennes, the enemies of his Crow tribe. In the fall of 1876 the army built its cantonment on the mouth of the Tongue River and in the ensuing winter Colonel Miles waged a campaign against the Sioux and Cheyennes along the Yellowstone. It is during this campaign that John Ermine rode for reinforcements and Wolf-Voice complained of fighting in the cold. On 25 November of that cold winter Colonel Ranald Mackenzie and 1,100 men attacked a Cheyenne village in a canyon on a fork of the Powder River and ultimately drove the Cheyennes into the mountains. This was the battle in which Fire-Eater, the hero of *The Way,* lost his medicine and waited for "the evil spirits to come and take him." It was in this cold winter that Sun-Down Leflare carried Order No. 6 from Keogh to St. Buford and Ermine and Wolf-Voice carried a message to Fort Keogh.

Remington wanted his novel to be not only historically accurate but also to be in accord with the scientific theories of his day. He read popular works on social evolution and subscribed to contemporary attitudes about race, atavism, and phrenology. In this he was not alone. The literature of the nineteenth century is littered with words, phrases, tedious paragraphs, even story plots that came from science and today are read as metaphor or poetic construct. The word *galvanize,* for example, derives from the work of Luigi Galvani (1737–1798) and his experiments with electricity. Frankenstein's monster was "galvanized" into life in 1817. Galvani also developed a theory of the generation of electricity in animals, including man, so that when Walt Whitman sang of the body electric, he had the authority of science behind him. When a political scientist spoke of the body politic, he could quite solemnly give the organs of the body that performed the separate functions of government.

The superiority of the white race was taken for granted, but some were more equal than others. The village Indians in *John Ermine* observed that White Weasel had exceptional fortitude for a white person, and wondered at it: "Any white man could see at a glance that White Weasel was evolved from a race which, however remote from him, got its yellow hair, fair skin, and blue eyes amidst the fjords, forests, rocks, and ice-floes of the north of Europe. The fierce sun of lower latitudes had burned no ancestor of Weasel's; their skins had been protected by the hides of animals" (*CW,* 464). Weasel was not merely a white boy, but a superior one descended from Norsemen.

Alexander Nemerov, dealing primarily with Remington's art, points to the evidence of Remington's belief in social evolution, that is, in the progress of man from bestial savage to a more humane and peaceful stage, and the assumption that such progress will continue:

The work that most graphically illustrates Remington's interest in evolution is a little-known sculpture, *Paleolithic Man,* from 1806. The sculpture shows a crouching prehistoric man holding a club in one hand and a clam shell in the other as he stares intently . . . from the mouth of a cave. With his strange appearance . . . he is an evolutionary prototype of a human being. Moreover, his rudimentary activity, cracking open clams with a stick, tells us that his way of gathering food (and his technological knowledge generally) is primitive. It was not for nothing that Remington gave a copy of the sculpture to his friend Theodore Roosevelt, himself a staunch evolutionist historian.[4]

Evolution may have its obverse, as Remington shows when Ermine finally returns to kill Lieutenant Butler. "All the patient training of Crooked Bear, all the humanizing influence of white association, all softening moods of the pensive face in the photograph, were blown from the fugitive as though carried on a wind; he was a shellfish-eating cave-dweller, with a Springfield, a knife, and a revolver. He had ceased to think in English and muttered to himself in Absaroke" (*CW,* 548). Here Remington is invoking what he would regard as scientific theory, namely atavism, the reversion of an individual to a more primitive stage of existence.

The "science" of phrenology dealt with individual organs of the brain that were responsible for specific faculties or traits of character; the size of bumps and the contours of the skull indicated the size of the organ underneath. Crooked Bear had pointed to his own forehead to indicate where the white man's medicine was lodged. John Ermine, true to the teachings of phrenology, learns to speak English very quickly. "The broad forehead responded promptly to the strain put upon it. Before the snows came, the two had rarely to use the harsh language of the tribesmen" (*CW,* 482). Remington's readers would have recognized in the references to the broad foreheads that the boy and Crooked Bear had exceptionally well developed organs essential to language and the sciences.

Some elements in *John Ermine* suggest reflections of Remington's life. Growing up, he was close to his father, enjoying hanging about their horses and racing stables. Growing up among the Indians, little White Weasel loves looking after his father's horses. Weasel enjoys an active childhood, reflecting Remington's own boyish pleasures. Little Indian boys "are very much like little white boys in every respect, except that they are subject to no restraint, and carry their mischievousness to all bounds" (*CW,* 463). They swim, they play war games, they hunt marmots, they tease old women, and in this rough play, White Weasel is the leader, as young Remington himself had been in Canton.

In his lessons from Crooked Bear, White Weasel does well in arithmetic, geography, and the sciences, while Remington himself disliked those subjects, perhaps now vicariously succeeding through his young prototype. White Weasel is excited by the tales of "ten thousand men in a single battle of the Great White Man's war" (*CW,* 488). In his school days, young Frederic was thrilled by Froissart's chronicles of battles with dead men by the thousands.

More important in Remington's life was the untimely death of his father when Remington was not yet 20. *John Ermine* has a series of surrogate fathers in the novel, much as Remington became fond of figures like General Miles to replace the dashing soldier he had loved and admired. Ermine's Indian foster father is a benign figure, kind to the boy and self-sacrificing in giving him up to Crooked Bear. The hermit then treats the boy with fatherly affection. When Ermine becomes an army scout, Major Searles takes a special interest in him and is called "Uncle" by the young scout. Remington's own uncles were surrogate fathers to him for many years.

Crooked Bear teaches the boy the Christian religion without the "mystery." He changes White Weasel's name to John Ermine, a name that would have "no Indian mystery about it." Then he stepped "from his Indian pedestal," announced that he was "no prophet; he was only a man. . . . He told the story of Jesus, and had John Ermine repeat the Ten Commandments" (*CW,* 483). This is the rationalist religion of Grandfather Remington's Universalist Church ministry. The young John Ermine was keeping the mystery of one religion and the morality of the other.

If there is a mythic and literary model for John Ermine, it might well be the Welsh Percival, the fatherless youth who rides forth armed with precepts from his mother (which get him into trouble), travels a dangerous road to King Arthur's court, performs noble deeds, has adventures at court (not all pleasant), and meets a dangerous woman. Out of this tale came such figures as Cervantes' Don Quixote and Dumas's D'Artagnan. It is a story that can run to tragedy or comedy, and even in comedy it is bittersweet. It is a story that may be set in the West, with characters Indian or white. Some of the virtues of its hero may be virtues of the mythic Western: innocence, simplicity, honesty, masculinity. John Seelye also finds in Ermine an illustration of R. W. B. Lewis's mythic American Adam and notes affinities with Melville's Christ-figure, Billy

Budd, and with Natty Bumppo of Cooper's Leatherstocking tales (Seelye, 254).

John Ermine of the Yellowstone came out on 12 November 1902, and within three weeks Macmillan was going to press with a second edition. Altogether Remington netted about $4,000 in royalties and felt that his novel had met with a modest success, although it did not match the spectacular popularity of Wister's *The Virginian.* The reviews were mixed but generally favorable, and in the following year, his friend Louis Shipman produced a play on Broadway based on the novel. To Remington's amused dismay, the play catered to popular taste by adding a happy ending. Neither the leading actor nor the production pleased Remington, but he and Eva were delighted with the whole experience of being a part of the New York theater world.

John Ermine was Remington's last literary effort. As the Samuels put it, "Remington realized that *John Ermine* was his best shot. If *Ermine* was not good enough to beat Wister or Garland, then he was better off spending his dreaming time on bronzes like 'Coming Through the Rye' or on the series of paintings he had in mind as the ultimate statement of Western history" (336).

The novel was a remarkable achievement for a man who was primarily an artist and who dashed it off in three months in the summer. He had accomplished his goal of writing a "real" novel and could turn with satisfaction back to his true vocation.

Afterword

From the beginning, Frederic Remington was identified with the wild West, a geographical area on the plains of the Southwest and in the northern country of Wyoming and Montana. In the Age of Reform, America's literary attention shifted to a different West: the economic West of Chicago and California in Frank Norris's *The Octopus* (1901) and *The Pit* (1903), and to the agrarian Midwest of Hamlin Garland and Willa Cather. Jack London, with *The Son of the Wolf: Tales of the Far North* (1900), had staked out a new frontier in the Klondike gold rush and turned stories of the strenuous life into parables of class struggle. In the year of Remington's death, 1909, London published his autobiographical *Martin Eden* and moved Bret Harte's San Francisco into the modern capitalist world. In that same year, Zane Grey published *The Last Trail,* and Remington's wild West was on its way to becoming the scene of the formula Western, with its errant gunman. In such a milieu, Remington's popularity declined.

It was not until the 1940s that interest in Remington revived along with the critical reexamination of the West, exemplified in literature by such works as Walter van Tilburg Clark's *The Ox-Bow Incident* (1940) and A. B. Guthrie's *The Big Sky* (1947). In the 1950s the trend continued with the "adult" Western, which broke with the formula. Films such as *Shane,* starring Alan Ladd, and *The Gunfighter,* starring Gregory Peck, portrayed the gunman as a tragic rather than a triumphant figure.

In the years following Remington's death in 1909, his reputation as an artist was never entirely obscured, but published commentary on his writing was virtually nonexistent.[1] In 1947 Harold McCracken published the first full-length biography of Remington, *Frederic Remington: Artist of the Old West,*[2] including a checklist of books by and about Remington. Although McCracken's primary interest was in Remington's art, he took into account his writing as well.

In the 1960s reprints of Remington's writings began to appear. Harold McCracken's *Frederic Remington's Own West* made available 26 pieces from his magazine publications.[3] In 1961, the University of Oklahoma reprinted Remington's *Pony Tracks* in a series devoted to the Western frontier.[4] *John Ermine of the Yellowstone* appeared in 1968 in a series titled "Americans in Fiction" from the Gregg Press,[5] featuring works no longer in print but of interest to literary historians.

By the 1970s the academic community began to pay critical attention to Remington as a writer. Ben Merchant Vorpahl made an important contribution to Remington scholarship in *My Dear Wister: The Frederic Remington–Owen Wister Letters*. Not limited merely to a collection of the correspondence between the two men, Vorpahl's book ranges over the biographical and literary contexts in which they lived and wrote. This was followed by the first close analysis of Remington's writings in Vorpahl's *Frederic Remington and the West: With the Eye of the Mind*.[6]

The year 1979 saw the advent of Peggy and Harold Samuels, whose work became the foundation for all subsequent work on Remington. *The Collected Writings of Frederic Remington* made available for the first time his articles in the major journals of his day, as well as his fiction, including complete texts of both novels. Three years later came their definitive work, *Frederic Remington: A Biography*. Although as art historians the Samuels focus on Remington's life as artist, they by no means neglect his writing, including in both areas of his life an abundance of material not previously known.[7] Another collection, *Frederic Remington: Selected Writings*, appeared in 1981, with an introduction by the Samuels.[8] In 1988 Allen and Marilyn Splete published *Frederic Remington: Selected Letters*, including commentary for each chapter and many charming sketches with which Remington decorated his letters. The 1980s and '90s have continued to see books on Remington the artist, many with splendid illustrations in color.

So, what is Remington's legacy as a writer? There is little doubt that Remington the artist has a strong claim to fame. His accomplishments in drawing, painting, and sculpture place him beyond the label of merely a "Western" artist. As a writer, he belongs to that second rank whose works have value and pertinence as lively reflections of the times in which he lived.

It may well be that Remington as a writer will be chiefly associated with the West, but he may also hold a place in American literature among that group of young turn-of-the-century writers, mostly journalists, who wrote outside the genteel tradition, such men as Stephen Crane, John Fox Jr., O. Henry, Jack London, John G. Neihardt (before he became an epic poet), Frank Norris, and playwright Augustus Thomas. These were the avant-garde of the gaslight era.

Remington rode and talked and sported with a wide range of men. He was interested in what men did to make a living and to make life enjoyable. He gave praise in his writing to the man who did what he was expected to do and did it well: the enterprising field officer, the trooper, the vaquero, or the French Canadian guide. With a lean, packed style, he created dramatic situations featuring colorful men in action. There is a lasting sincerity and veracity in his writing because he chose not to paint the big picture but rather to catch the simple heroism of an incident: a scout carrying a message through a hostile land or a band of Indians making a last stand in the dead of winter. He witnessed the last of the Indian wars, the last big ranch rodeos, and the last glorious days of the cavalry. He wrote with a unique brand of gritty realism, romantic sentiment, good humor, and strong personal opinion that made him one of the most popular writers of his day and well worth the respect and attention of today's readers.

Notes and References

Chapter One

1. Peggy Samuels and Harold Samuels, *Frederic Remington: A Biography* (New York: Doubleday, 1982; reprint, Austin: Univ. of Texas Press, 1985); hereafter cited in text as Samuels. This excellent and comprehensive work is the principal source for information on the life of Remington.

2. Frederic Remington, *The Collected Writings of Frederic Remington,* ed. Peggy Samuels and Harold Samuels (Garden City, N.Y.: Doubleday, 1979), 599; hereafter cited in text as *CW.*

Chapter Two

1. Darwin Payne, *Owen Wister: Chronicler of the West, Gentleman of the East* (Dallas: Southern Methodist Univ. Press, 1985), 29.

2. The title refers to the name the Cheyennes called themselves.

3. This incident is the subject of Mari Sandoz's *Cheyenne Autumn* (New York: Avon, 1964).

4. Ben Merchant Vorpahl, *My Dear Wister: The Frederic Remington–Owen Wister Letters* (Palo Alto, Calif.: American West, 1972), 279; hereafter cited in text.

Chapter Three

1. Boston: Houghton Mifflin, 1959.

2. Robert M. Utley, *Frontier Regulars: The United States Army and the Indian, 1866–1891* (Lincoln: Univ. of Nebraska Press, 1973), 275–76; hereafter cited in text.

3. Brian W. Dippie, " 'What Valor Is': Artists and the Mythic Moment," *Montana: The Magazine of Western History* 46 (Autumn 1996): 40–55. Shows Remington's three drawings of the battle.

4. Ben Merchant Vorpahl, *Frederic Remington and the West: With the Eye of the Mind* (Austin: Univ. of Texas Press, 1978), 275; hereafter cited in text.

5. John Seelye, "Frederic Remington: The Writer," in *Frederic Remington: The Masterworks,* ed. Michael Edward Shapiro and Peter H. Hassrick (New York: Abrams, 1991), 242; hereafter cited in text.

Chapter Four

1. Allen P. Splete and Marilyn D. Splete, *Frederic Remington: Selected Letters* (New York: Abbeville Press, 1988), 157; hereafter cited in text.

2. Frank Marryat, *Mountains and Molehills: Recollections of a Burnt Journal,* ed. Robin W. Winks (Philadelphia: Lippincott, 1962), 45–46.

3. New York: Arno and the *New York Times,* 1969, 15.

4. The complete text of Wister's "The Evolution of the Cow-Puncher" is included in Vorpahl's *My Dear Wister.* For the reader's convenience, all citations are from this source.

Chapter Five

1. *A New Collection of Thomas Bangs Thorpe's Sketches of the Old Southwest,* ed. David C. Estes (Baton Rouge: Louisiana State Univ. Press, 1989), 11.

2. Edmund Morris, *The Rise of Theodore Roosevelt* (New York: Coward, McCann and Geoghegan, 1979), 383–84.

Chapter Six

1. Max Lerner, *The Mind and Faith of Justice Holmes: His Speeches, Essays, Letters, and Judicial Opinions* (Boston: Little, Brown, 1951), 18; hereafter cited in text.

2. Owen Wister, "To the Reader," *The Virginian: The Horseman of the Plains* (Boston: Houghton Mifflin, 1968), 4.

3. See Mari Sandoz, *The Cattlemen: From the Rio Grande across the Far Marias* (Lincoln: Univ. of Nebraska Press, 1978), 492–96.

4. M. R. Bennett, *So Gallantly Streaming* (New York: Drake, 1974), 27.

5. See Douglas Allen, *Frederic Remington and the Spanish-American War* (New York: Crown, 1971), for newspaper clippings as well as Remington's illustrations of the period.

6. Virgil Carrington Jones, *Roosevelt's Rough Riders* (New York: Doubleday, 1971), 17.

7. John Fox was the future author of *The Little Shepherd of Kingdom Come* (1903) and *The Trail of the Lonesome Pine* (1908).

8. The Samuels point out that Remington was "bumming" food for several days when the men were on half-rations and that that had more to do with his being ostracized than did purchasing a horse (Samuels, 278–79).

9. Remington's double-page plate *The Storming of San Juan: The Head of the Charge* appeared in *Harper's Weekly* (6 August 1898).

10. Richard Harding Davis, *Notes of a War Correspondent* (New York: Scribner's, 1911), 99.

Chapter Seven

1. The text of *John Ermine* is included in the *Collected Writings,* and all quotations are from that source.

2. Fred Erisman, *Frederic Remington* (Boise, Idaho: Boise State Univ., 1975), 31.

3. Clarence Ghodes, introduction to *John Ermine of the Yellowstone,* by Frederic Remington (Ridgewood, N.J.: Gregg Press, 1968), no p.

4. Alexander Nemerov, *Frederic Remington and Turn of the Century America* (New Haven: Yale Univ. Press, 1995), 10.

Afterword

1. See Peter H. Hassrick, "Frederic Remington: The Painter," *Montana: The Magazine of Western History* 40 (Summer 1996): 18–35, for an excellent summary of art criticism on Remington.

2. Philadelphia: Lippincott, 1947.

3. New York: Dial, 1960.

4. New York: Harper, 1895; reprint, Norman: Univ. of Oklahoma Press, 1961.

5. New York: Macmillan, 1902; reprint, Ridgewood, N.J.: Gregg Press, 1968.

6. Austin: Univ. of Texas Press, 1978.

7. They give evidence, for example, that *John Ermine of the Yellowstone* was Remington's second novel, not his first, as earlier writers had assumed because of the later publication date of *The Way of an Indian.*

8. Secaucus, N.J.: Castle, 1981.

Selected Bibliography

PRIMARY SOURCES

Collected Writings of Frederic Remington. Edited by Peggy Samuels and Harold Samuels. Garden City, N.Y.: Doubleday, 1979. Invaluable for access to Remington's writings. Includes illustrations and useful notes.

Crooked Trails. New York: Harper, 1898. Second anthology of *Harper's* articles.

Frederic Remington: Selected Writings. Compiled by Frank Oppel. Secaucus, N.J.: Castle, 1981. Photocopies of 43 essays and stories from original magazines, including illustrations. No dates or commentary.

John Ermine of the Yellowstone. New York: Macmillan, 1902. Reprint, Ridgewood, N.J.: Gregg Press, 1968.

Men with the Bark On. New York: Harper, 1900. Fourth anthology of *Harper's* articles.

Pony Tracks. New York: Harper, 1895. First anthology of *Harper's* articles.

A Rogers Ranger in the French and Indian War. New York: Harper, 1897. A reprint of the short story "Joshua Goodenough's Old Letter" (*Harper's Monthly,* November 1897).

Stories of Peace and War. New York: Harper, 1899. Third anthology of *Harper's* articles.

Sun-Down Leflare. New York: Harper, 1899. Five stories.

The Way of an Indian. New York: Fox Duffield, 1906.

SECONDARY SOURCES

Books and Parts of Books

Allen, Douglas. *Frederic Remington and the Spanish-American War.* New York: Crown, 1971. Includes illustrations, news clippings, and texts of some of Remington's articles on the war.

Ballinger, James K. *Frederic Remington.* New York: Abrams, in association with the Natural Museum of American Art, Smithsonian Institute, 1989.

Beer, Thomas. *The Mauve Decade: American Life at the End of the Nineteenth Century.* New York: Knopf, 1926.

Bennett, M. R. *So Gallantly Streaming.* New York: Drake, 1974.

Cashin, Hershel V. *Under Fire with the 10th U.S. Cavalry.* New York: F. Tennyson Nealy, 1898. Reprinted in the series The American Negro: His History and Literature. New York: Arno Press and the *New York Times,* 1969.

Davis, Richard Harding. *Notes of a War Correspondent.* New York: Scribner's, 1911.

Davis, Ronald J. *Augustus Thomas*. Boston: Twayne, 1984.

Dippie, Brian W. *Remington and Russell*. Austin: Univ. of Texas Press, 1982. The art of two Western painters. Illustrated.

Dunlay, Thomas W. *Wolves for the Blue Soldiers: Indian Scouts and Auxiliaries with the United States Army, 1860–1890*. Lincoln: Univ. of Nebraska Press, 1982.

Dunne, Finley Peter. *Mr. Dooley in Peace and War*. Boston: Small, Maynard, 1898.

Erisman, Fred. *Frederic Remington*. Boise State Univ. Western Writers Series, no. 16. Boise, Idaho: Boise State Univ. Press, 1975.

Etulain, Howard. *Re-imagining the American West: A Century of Fiction, History, and Art*. Tucson: Univ. of Arizona Press, 1996.

Etulain, Howard, and N. Jill Howard, eds. *A Bibliographic Guide to Western American Literature*. Albuquerque: Univ. of New Mexico Press, 1995.

Ewers, John C. *Artists of the Old West*. Garden City, N.Y.: Doubleday, 1973. Analysis of Remington and relationship with Indian warfare.

Hassrick, Peter H. *Frederic Remington: Paintings, Drawings, and Sculpture in the Amon Carter Museum and the Sid Richardson Foundation Collection*. New York: Wings Books, 1973. Foreword by Ruth Carter Johnson. Large reproductions, many in color. Text and commentary by Hassrick.

Hassrick, Peter H., and Melissa J. Webster. *Frederic Remington: A Catalogue Raisonné of Paintings, Watercolors, and Drawings*. 2 vols. Cody, Wyo.: Buffalo Bill Historical Center, 1996.

Hultkrantz, Aka. *Native Religions of North America: The Power of Visions and Fertility*. New York: Harper and Row, 1987.

James, Marquis. *The Cherokee Strip: An Oklahoma Boyhood*. New York: Viking, 1945. The land run in September 1893, 54–63.

Jones, Virgil Carrington. *Roosevelt's Rough Riders*. Garden City, N.Y.: Doubleday, 1971.

Larkin, Oliver W. *Art and Life in America*. New York: Reinhart, 1949.

Leckie, William H. *The Buffalo Soldiers: A Narrative of the Negro Cavalry in the West*. Norman: Univ. of Oklahoma Press, 1967.

Lerner, Max, ed. *The Mind and Faith of Justice Holmes*. Boston: Little, Brown, 1951. Patriotic speech at Harvard University, 1895, 18–27.

London, Jack. *Sporting Blood: Selections from Jack London's Greatest Sports Writing*. Novato, Calif.: Presidio Press, 1981.

Lott, Milton. *Dance Back the Buffalo*. Boston: Houghton Mifflin, 1959.

———. *The Last Hunt*. Boston: Houghton Mifflin, 1954.

Manley, Atwood. *Frederic Remington in the Land of His Youth*. Ogdensburg, N.Y.: Northern New York Pub. Co., 1961.

Marryat, Frank. *Mountains and Molehills: or, Recollections of a Burnt Journal*, ed. Robin W. Winks. London: Longmans, 1855. Reprint, Philadelphia: Lippincott, 1962. An Englishman's travels in the American West in mid-century.

Marshall, Edward. *The Story of the Rough Riders*. New York: Dillingham, 1899.

McCracken, Harold. *Frederic Remington: Artist of the Old West*. Philadelphia: Lippincott, 1947.

————, ed. *Frederic Remington's Own West*. New York: Dial, 1960. Twenty-six selections of Remington's writings.

McCullough, David G. *Brave Companions: Portraits in History*. New York: Prentice Hall, 1992.

Millis, Walter. *The Martial Spirit: A Study of Our War with Spain*. Boston: Houghton Mifflin, 1931.

Morris, Edmund. *The Rise of Theodore Roosevelt*. New York: Coward, McCann and Geoghegan, 1979.

Musicani, Ivan. *Empire by Default: The Spanish-American War and the Dawn of the American Century*. New York: Holt, 1998.

Nemerov, Alexander. *Frederic Remington and Turn of the Century America*. New Haven, Conn.: Yale Univ. Press, 1995. Focus is on Remington as artist.

Payne, Darwin. *Owen Wister: Chronicler of the West, Gentleman of the East*. Dallas: Southern Methodist Univ. Press, 1985.

Rogers, W. A. *A World Worth While: A Record of "Auld Acquaintance."* New York: Harper, 1922. Rogers was Harper's art editor; personal recollections of Remington.

Roosevelt, Theodore. *An Autobiography*. New York, Macmillan, 1913. Reprint, New York: Da Capo Press, 1985. Introduction by Etting Morison.

————. *Ranch Life and the Hunting-Trail*. 1888. Reprint, New York: Arno and the *New York Times,* 1970.

————. *The Rough Riders*. New York: Collier, 1899.

Rush, Arwin N. *Frederic Remington and Owen Wister*. Tallahassee: Florida State Univ. Press, 1961.

Samuels, Peggy, and Harold Samuels. *Frederic Remington: A Biography*. New York: Macmillan, 1982. Reprint, Austin: Univ. of Texas, 1985. A comprehensive and definitive work. Although the method of citation is somewhat unorthodox, all sources are identified. Refreshingly readable.

Sandoz, Mari. *The Cattlemen: From the Rio Grande across the Far Marias*. Lincoln: Univ. of Nebraska Press, 1958.

————. *Cheyenne Autumn*. New York: Avon, 1964.

Savage, W. Sherman. *Blacks in the West*. Contributions in Afro-American and African Studies, no. 23. Westport, Conn.: Greenwood Press, 1976.

Seelye, John. "Frederick Remington: The Writer." In *Frederic Remington: The Masterworks,* ed. Michael Edward Shapiro and Peter H. Hassrick. New York: Harry N. Abrams, 1991.

Shapiro, Michael Edward, and Peter H. Hassrick, eds. *Frederic Remington: The Masterworks*. New York: Harry N. Abrams, 1991. Illustrations, many in color.

Smith, Henry Nash. *Virgin Land: The American West as Symbol and Myth*. New York: Vintage Books, 1957.

Splete, Allen P., and Marilyn D. Splete. *Frederic Remington: Selected Letters.* New York: Abbeville Press, 1988. Includes many of Remington's sketches in the letters. Excellent introductory essays to each chapter.

Strong, Josiah. *Our Country: Its Possible and Its Present Crisis.* 2nd ed. New York: Baker and Taylor, 1891.

Swanberg, W. A. *Citizen Hearst.* New York: Bantam Books, 1961.

Thorpe, Thomas Bangs. *A New Collection of Thomas Bangs Thorpe's Sketches of the Old Southwest.* Edited by David C. Estes. Baton Rouge: Louisiana State Univ. Press, 1989.

Tompkins, Jane. *West of Everything: The Inner Life of Westerns.* New York: Oxford Univ. Press, 1992.

Utley, Robert M. *Frontier Regulars: The United States Army and the Indian, 1866–1891.* Lincoln: Univ. of Nebraska Press, 1973.

Vorpahl, Ben Merchant. *Frederic Remington and the West: With the Eye of the Mind.* Austin: Univ. of Texas Press, 1978. Major critical study. (The format of marginal notes without a bibliography is inconvenient.)

————. *My Dear Wister: The Frederic Remington–Owen Wister Letters.* Palo Alto, Calif.: American West, 1972. Foreword by Wallace Stegner. Biographical and critical material throughout each chapter.

Westermeier, Clifford P. *Who Rush to Glory: The Cowboy Volunteers of 1898: Grigsby's Cowboys, Roosevelt's Rough Riders, Torrey's Rocky Mountain Riders.* Caldwell, Idaho: Caxton Printers, 1958.

Wharfield, Colonel H. B. *10th Cavalry and Border Fights.* El Cajon, California: privately printed, 1965.

White, G. Edward. *The Eastern Establishment and the Western Experience: The West of Frederic Remington, Theodore Roosevelt, and Owen Wister.* New Haven, Conn.: Yale Univ. Press, 1968.

Wister, Owen. *The Virginian: The Horseman of the Plains.* Boston: Houghton Mifflin, 1968.

Ziff, Larzer. *The American 1890's: Life and Times of a Lost Generation.* New York: Viking, 1966.

Articles

Allen, E. Douglas. "Frederic Remington—Author and Illustrator: A List of His Contributions to American Periodicals." *Bulletin of the New York Public Library* 49 (December 1945): 895–912.

Dippie, Brian W. "Reflections on a Reputation: The Remington Raisonné." *Montana: The Magazine of Western History* 47 (Summer 1997): 69–74.

————. " 'What Valor Is': Artists and the Mythic Moment." *Montana: The Magazine of Western History* 46 (Autumn 1966): 40–55. Remington's drawings of Custer's last stand.

Gates, John Morgan. "General George Crook's First Apache Campaign." *Journal of the West* 6 (April 1967): 310–20.

Hassrick, Peter H. "Frederic Remington the Painter: A Historiographical Sketch." *Montana: The Magazine of Western History* 46 (Summer 1996): 18–35.

Robinson, Forrest G. "The Roosevelt—Wister Connection." *Western American Literature* 14 (Summer 1979): 95–114.

West, Elliott. "Called Out People: The Cheyennes and the Central Plains." *Montana: The Magazine of Western History* 48 (Summer 1998): 2–15.

White, Lonnie J. "Indian Battles in the Texas Panhandle, 1874." *Journal of the West* 6 (April 1967): 278–309.

Index

The Author

Roscoe L. Buckland received his B.A. and M.A. in English at the University of Idaho in 1948 and his Ph.D. in American Studies at the University of Iowa in 1955. He has taught at Washington State University, served as Chair of English at California State University at Long Beach, and served as Chair of Liberal Studies at Western Washington University. He taught as a University Exchange Professor at Asia University in Tokyo in 1985. He has published on Bret Hart and Owen Wister and has reviewed nineteenth-century literature for *Western American Literature* and for *Studies in Short Fiction.* He was a founding member of the Western Literature Association, reading papers and serving on panels at the annual meetings. Since his retirement he has maintained his interest in frontier history and literature.

The Editor

Joseph M. Flora earned his B.A. (1956), M.A. (1957), and Ph.D. (1962) in English at the University of Michigan. In 1962 he joined the faculty of the University of North Carolina, where he is professor of English. His study *Hemingway's Nick Adams* (1984) won the Mayflower Award. He is also author of *Vardis Fisher* (1962), *William Ernest Henley* (1970), *Frederick Manfred* (1974), and *Ernest Hemingway: A Study of the Short Fiction* (1989). He is editor of *The English Short Story* (1985) and coeditor of *Southern Writers: A Biographical Dictionary* (1970), *Fifty Southern Writers before 1900* (1987), and *Fifty Southern Writers after 1900* (1987). He serves on the editorial boards of *Studies in Short Fiction* and *Southern Literary Journal*.